T0360459

Human Resource Management and the Implementation of Change

With the increased pace of global, economical and technological development, change has become an inevitable feature of any organisation to survive in the competitive market. If it is a planned change process, the HR practitioner can use any of the existing general models or theories of change and use suggestive interventions to increase effectiveness and capability to change itself. When the magnitude of change is unpredictable or the degree of the organisational process or systems is unorganised, the existing models or practice of planned change is still in the formative stage, and there is room for continuous refinement and improvement.

This book will bridge this gap in the current organisational development and change literature by benefiting the HR practitioner with six real case studies. The cases bring out the interventions adopted, key activities associated with the successful implementation of interventions and the critical role played by HR in achieving organisational effectiveness. This book captures the transformational journey of a diverse set of companies and weaves various dimensions into a common coherent framework for the field of HRM in Change Management. The case studies illustrate six powerful organisational experiences, listing the major activities contributing to effective change management from motivating change, vision, support from key stakeholders, transition management to organisational and HR commitment for implementation.

By demonstrating the role of HR as a 'change agent,' this volume will be valuable to researchers, academics, managers and students in the fields of human resource management and change management.

Dr. Paritosh Mishra is Professor of Human Resources, Organisational Behaviour and Industrial Relations at Amity Business School, Amity University, Noida, Uttar Pradesh, India.

Dr. Balvinder Shukla is Vice Chancellor and Professor of Entrepreneurship and Leadership at Amity University, Noida, Uttar Pradesh, India.

Dr. R. Sujatha is Professor of HR and Entrepreneurship at Amity Business School, Amity University, Noida, Uttar Pradesh, India.

Routledge Focus on Business and Management

The fields of business and management have grown exponentially as areas of research and education. This growth presents challenges for readers trying to keep up with the latest important insights. *Routledge Focus on Business and Management* presents small books on big topics and how they intersect with the world of business research.

Individually, each title in the series provides coverage of a key academic topic, whilst collectively, the series forms a comprehensive collection across the business disciplines.

Optimal Spending on Cybersecurity Measures
Risk Management
Tara Kissoon

Small Business, Big Government and the Origins of Enterprise Policy
The UK Bolton Committee
Robert Wapshott and Oliver Mallett

Conflict, Power, and Organizational Change
Deborah A. Colwill

Human Resource Management for Organisational Change
Theoretical Formulations
Dr. Paritosh Mishra, Dr. Balvinder Shukla and Dr. R. Sujatha

Human Resource Management and the Implementation of Change
Dr. Paritosh Mishra, Dr. Balvinder Shukla and Dr. R. Sujatha

Corporate Governance Models
A Critical Assessment
Marco Mastrodascio

For more information about this series, please visit: www.routledge.com/ Routledge-Focus-on-Business-and-Management/book-series/FBM

Human Resource Management and the Implementation of Change

Dr. Paritosh Mishra,
Dr. Balvinder Shukla and
Dr. R. Sujatha

Routledge
Taylor & Francis Group

NEW YORK AND LONDON

First published 2022
by Routledge
605 Third Avenue, New York, NY 10158

and by Routledge
2 Park Square, Milton Park, Abingdon, Oxon, OX14 4RN

Routledge is an imprint of the Taylor & Francis Group, an informa business

Library of Congress Cataloging-in-Publication Data
Names: Mishra, Paritosh, 1962– author. | Shukla, Balvinder, author. |
    Sujatha, R. (Independent researcher), author.
Title: Human resource management and the implementation of change /
    Dr. Paritosh Mishra, Dr. Balvinder Shukla and Dr. R. Sujatha.
Description: New York, NY : Routledge, 2022. | Series: Routledge focus
    on business and management | Includes bibliographical references
    and index.
Identifiers: LCCN 2021031826 (print) | LCCN 2021031827 (ebook) |
    ISBN 9781032042992 (hardback) | ISBN 9781032043029 (paperback) |
    ISBN 9781003191384 (ebook)
Subjects: LCSH: Organizational change. | Personnel management. |
    Human capital.
Classification: LCC HD58.8 .M567 2022 (print) | LCC HD58.8 (ebook) |
    DDC 658.4/06—dc23
LC record available at https://lccn.loc.gov/2021031826
LC ebook record available at https://lccn.loc.gov/2021031827

ISBN: 978-1-032-04299-2 (hbk)
ISBN: 978-1-032-04302-9 (pbk)
ISBN: 978-1-003-19138-4 (ebk)

DOI: 10.4324/9781003191384

Typeset in Times New Roman
by Apex CoVantage, LLC

Contents

Figures

Tables

Acknowledgements

This book is an anthology of case studies and such an anthology would not be possible without the support of industry leaders to carry out the research. Our sincere thanks go to Mr. Gurdeep Singh, CMD, NTPC, Mr. Sankaran Subramaniam, Ex-MD, OPGC, Mr. Rajeev Bhadauria, Ex- Group Director (HR), JSPL, Mr. Debabrata Mohapatra, Ex-Head (HR), L&T (E&A), Mr. Barttanu Das, Ex-Sr. Vice President (HR), Blue Dart, and Mr. Amiya Pattanayak, Ex-GM(HR), NALCO, for having given permission to carry out research in their companies. Further, this study would not have been completed without the honest input of all those interviewed in these companies and we profusely thank them for the same.

We wish to thank the reviewers who have painstakingly reviewed our draft versions by taking time out of their busy schedules and giving critical suggestions regarding improving the structure, content and format of the book. Only by complying with the hundreds of suggestions of the reviewers, the book could reach its current shape.

Our sincere thanks go to Amity University Uttar Pradesh who have kindly consented to the publication of the book. We sincerely acknowledge the support and encouragement given by friends and colleagues during the endeavour to complete this book.

We acknowledge the co-operation and understanding of our family members extended to us during this period, but for which this endeavour would not have come to fruition. Our love and thanks to Smruti, Suren, and Ram, from the bottom of our hearts. We also thank one another. We have learned a lot through our process of research and writing books together.

Preface

This book provides a comprehensive, research-based, integrated perspective of Change Interventions and Human Resource Management. This book makes an exposition of organisational change in different facets and examines the role of HR in those divergent perspectives of Change Management. The book's comprehensiveness is evidenced by its wide coverage of dimensions and companies. In terms of typology, it takes up two Central Public Sector Undertakings, one Indian family business, two European multinational companies (one German and the other French) and one company which was a joint venture company on public-private partnership mode and which has since been turned into a 100% equity Odisha Government company.

In their earlier book *HR and Organisational Change: Theoretical Formulations*, the authors have brought out various theoretical formulations around change and its diverse facets and ramifications. In the said book, the authors have enunciated diverse models of organisational strategy, different dimensions of changing business environment and implications for HR, various theories of organisational change, theories and dimensions of resistance to change, concepts such as Organisational Culture and Leadership Styles with respect to their interconnections with organisational change and have put in perspective the evolving role of HR. They have also made an exposition of literature on High-Performance Work Practices (HPWP) to support change management in organisations and provided literature on a few HPWPs, such as Performance Management and Feedback Mechanisms, Building Competencies, HR Analytics, Participation in Decision Making Process and Building Value-based organisations.

With this book, the authors take their research to the next level by examining concrete Change interventions in Case Companies and scrutinising the concomitant support systems built by or in HR to bring about and sustain the changes.

Foreword

That "change is the only constant" is a common adage that is often emphatically enunciated by many business practitioners, in almost every forum. However, the truth hits us home, when it starts to impact us individually or jolts the ecosystem that we are an integral part of. "Human Resource Management and the Implementation of Change" is a sequel to the book, "Human Resource Management for Organisational Change: Theoretical Formulations". Whilst a lot has been written about change management and its impact on the various facets and organisation, the intersection between human resource management and change management needs closer examination. This book endeavours to dive deep into this facet, by intertwining learnings from six unique case studies. An outcome of extensive research work carried out over 6 years, the case studies highlight how change can be brought about seamlessly, by bringing together organisational and functional HR strategies and building accompanying support systems to enable effective execution.

Each of the case studies covers a unique dimension on how to manage change from an HR perspective. A very interesting chronicle on Blue Dart has been enunciated in the context of centralisation versus local adaptation, as the organisation goes through change resulting from an acquisition by a Global Player. In the study on NTPC, one of India's most respected government-owned entities, the authors examine the Organisational Transformation exercise called "Disha", with respect to strategy, at both the organisational and HR level. The evolving role of the Human Resource Management function in adopting professional practices is effectively studied in the context of Jindal Steel and Power Limited, a leading Indian Corporate. Another noteworthy study on developing healthy HRM practices to facilitate engagement with Trade Unions whilst adapting to the changing paradigm of employee relations is dutifully highlighted in the case study on NALCO. The role of HR in building support systems in the light of the "PADR" organisational strategy model is studied in the context of Schneider

Electric India Pvt. Ltd. Last, but not least of all, the authors examine the relevance of various Critical Success Factors (CSFs) alongside the multiple stages of implementation of SAP at OPGC. Technology truly plays an effective, multidimensional role.

Though the book is based on research of case studies across different firms from diverse sectors, industries and organisation types, it is not an unrelated conglomeration of disparate papers. All the chapters are coherently interconnected and constitute essential parts of a diligently built research agenda and collectively provide an insightful hypothesis to the field of Human Resource Management in the areas of change, transition and transformation.

This book attempts to quench the intellectual thirst of different sections of students and practitioners. Advanced undergraduate students and master's students will find this book useful as supplementary reading, as it gives a concise, albeit wide-ranging coverage of Change management and the role of HRM. For the doctoral and post-doctoral students and other researchers, this book provides a very good prologue to the field, as it offers cohesive coverage of the most recent theoretical developments in the diverse nuances of the changing nature of HR and its resultant systems and processes. As a research book, it provides an all-embracing list of references that will allow the researchers to obtain a state-of-the-art overview of the area. Business leaders and HR practitioners looking for solutions to their change management problems shall also find the book useful, as it is built on the framework of real-life case studies.

The language of the book is lucid and elegant, without being ornamental, and offers an enjoyable reading experience, whilst enunciating interesting facets of organisational change and transformation.

Enjoy!

Manoj Chugh
President – Group Public Affairs
Mahindra & Mahindra

Introduction

This is an ever-changing world. And change in the current age in the world has been much faster, bigger, discontinuous and disruptive. At each step, the future, even in a short-term horizon, appears shrouded in a vortex of ambiguity and enveloped in a thick speck of uncertainty. In the world of obscurities, organisations are confronted with cumulative uncertainties and challenges of gargantuan proportions, not just limited to national, economic or societal borders (Eisenhardt, Graebner, & Sonenshein, 2016; Ferraro, Etzion, & Gehman, 2015), but engulfing the whole world like a small village. Despite this cloud of confusion about the way people navigate into the future, there always appear to be myriads of possibilities, an exponential rise in the availability of options and variegated interpretations of people about the way they perceive these options.

Strategy, Alignment and Change

Strategy is a set of decisions through which a business integrates its managerial processes and capabilities with its business environment. The importance of a strategic fit between resources, strategies, environment (opportunities/threats) and performance emanates from its definition, which says "a strategy describes the fundamental characteristics of the match that an organisation achieves amongst its skills and resources and the opportunities and threats in its external environment that enables it to achieve its goals and objectives" (Chrisman, Hofer, & Boulton, 1988, p. 414).

Organisations plan their resource allocation in pursuance of their strategy to define organisational direction and to guide decisions to fructify their mission and objectives. Strategic planning gives a sense of direction to the organisation, sketches measurable objectives and guides decisions at the transactional levels on daily basis (Lawrie, Abdullah, Bragg, & Varlet, 2016). Organisations seek to achieve strategic alignment at both organisational and functional levels, across domains of execution, technology

DOI: 10.4324/9781003191384-1

adoption, service orientation and competitive viability (Reksoatmodjo, Hartono, Djunaedi, & Utomo, 2012).

Organisations require a successful, smart HR strategy, in alignment with organisational strategy, to cope up with the challenges of technological transformation. Changes at the levels of organisational structure, leadership style and implementation of human resource management would be required to allow HR departments to discharge a more strategic role in the overall organisational growth (Sivathanu & Pillai, 2018).

Several momentous changes are affecting the world in recent times. On the one hand, organisations have sought to realise improved operational efficiency and productivity, which can be achieved through digitisation, optimisation, production customisation, automation, adaptation and the like (Lu, 2017; Roblek, Meško, & Krapež, 2016) and the world has entered into a new phase of Industrial Revolution. On the other, typically demonstrating how intricate, yet intertwined the world has become, the current corona crisis has thrust upon the business world challenges of unparalleled proportions. Having delved into and having been forced to manage an uncharted territory, organisations have adjusted their workforce in technical, physical and socio-psychological dimensions as perceived never before. Organisations have modified their work structures and processes encompassing social, psychological, physical and technical arenas, hitherto unforeseen. These twin phenomena of Industry 4.0 and the COVID-19 Pandemic adequately explain the context of the modern-day business world to set the tone for discussions of the main theme of the book, that is, the role of Human Resource Management in organisational change.

Industry 4.0

The term Industry 4.0 (I4.0) was first mentioned in Germany in 2011 (Badri, Boudreau-Trudel, & Souissi, 2018; Ding, 2018; Rajput & Singh, 2018). The Fourth Industrial Revolution is still underway here and now, and its impact is not yet fully known (Cieśla & Kolny, 2019; Ghobakhloo, 2018). In fact, there is no consensually accepted definition for I4.0 yet. Even as Bär, Herbert-Hansen, and Khalid (2018) categorise I4.0 as a manifestation of rapid change in technology, Geißler, Häckel, Voit, and Übelhör (2019) associate I4.0 with certain technological advancements such as Internet of Things (IoT) and Cyber-Physical Systems (CPS). This rests on the conceptualisation that production systems can optimise themselves quite autonomously without human intervention, leveraging on integrated interconnectivity and huge data (Bonekamp & Sure, 2015). Frederico, Garza-Reyes, Anosike, and Kumar (2019) define I4.0 as including "cutting-edge and disruptive technologies" and Pfohl, Yahsi, and Kurnaz (2015) as "sum of all disruptive innovations derived and implemented in a value chain to address the trends of digitalization".

In order to leverage the benefits of I4.0, industries would have to manage several complexities (Pinzone et al., 2020), deal with comprehensive infrastructure (Lezzi, Lazoi, & Corallo, 2018) and implement new work organisation and design (Karodia, 2018).

Industry 4.0 would be characterised by highly differentiated and customised products and a well-coordinated combination of products and services. Thus, it would require continuous innovation and learning, dependent on people and the enterprise's capabilities (Shamim, Cang, Yu, & Li, 2016). There would be a requirement for seamless integration of business systems, organisational processes and manufacturing systems (Sishi & Telukdarie, 2020). Quite logically, enterprise resource planning (ERP) systems are considered the mainstay for Industry 4.0 (Haddara & Elragal, 2015; Stojkić, Veža, & Bošnjak, 2016).

The three industrial revolutions of the past not only impacted the production and business models, but also altered the skill requirements in future industries (Benešová & Tupa, 2017). From one industrial revolution to the other, some jobs evaporated like a morning mist and other new ones sprang up. Some skills became obsolete, while other new ones became invaluable. The fourth industrial revolution is considered no exception.

Industry 4.0 necessitates people to interact with algorithms and robotics in a digitised, networked and virtualised workplace (Richert et al., 2016). Such changes result in requirements for a unique and specialised skills set (Grzelczak, Kosacka, & Werner-Lewandowska, 2017; Kergroach, 2017). Thus, in this era of Industry 4.0, organisational performance would hinge on employees trained in the new technological systems and in managing teams of specialised technical experts, which in turn would necessitate such profiles as are highly scarce.

A significant gap between the current capability of employees and their evolving roles has seemingly become evident, which has been brought to the surface because of the enormous speed with which change has been created by Industry 4.0. This has necessitated a new and fresh look at talent development and talent management processes (Whysall, Owtram, & Brittain, 2019). In order to leverage the advantages of the opportunities of industry 4.0 and moderate the accompanying challenges, HR professionals need to shoulder roles of strategic business partners and talent managers, which would require in them HR competencies of strategic partners, imaginative innovators, change agents and people enablers (Dhanpat, Buthelezi, Joe, Maphela, & Shongwe, 2020).

The COVID-19 Pandemic

If one unfolds the rolled-up scrolls of the history of the human race, one would observe that the world has undergone several crises during different stages of history. These crises have sometimes been cleavages facing nations, twice having engulfed the entire world, so much so, having been christened as world wars, sporadically been revolutions that have restructured the socio-politics completely. Yet, some other times these have been challenges of contagious diseases.

The world was faced with a new virus christened COVID-19, a new mutation of the coronavirus family, with the proclamation of the first case in the Wuhan district of China on 1 December 2019. The discriminating features of COVID-19, as compared to the earlier encounters, are its geographical dispersion in terms of contagion and its casualties. On 11 March 2020, the World Health Organization (WHO) declared the occurrence of novel coronavirus (COVID-19) a global pandemic.

Pandemic, by its characterisation, implies a disease or a condition that spreads across countries and continents (Pandemics, 2020). In the absence of a medical solution or vaccine to the coronavirus, among the methods that got resorted to for handling the epidemic have been three-fold: isolation, or diseased persons being separated from non-infected individuals, quarantine and surveillance of contacts who have been exposed, but are not symptomatic and community containment involving social distancing and restriction of movement of the general public through interventions such as "stay at home orders" (Wilder-Smith & Freedman, 2020).

As country after country resorted to handling the crisis through lockdown, isolation, quarantine and voluntary social distancing, organisations were forced to continue with their operations mostly through remote working and work from home modalities. And this has had its own baggage to come with it. One inevitable consequence has been increased feelings of solitude and social exclusion among employees (Kopp, 2020; Robinson, 2020).

Employees like to work for organisations whose work atmospheres mirror the same values and culture as their personal desires and convictions (Kristof-Brown & Guay, 2011), and there is a level of congruence between the individual's characteristics and those of the organisation, alternatively known as person-environment fit (P-E fit) (Kristof, 1996). Even as employees experience increased job satisfaction, engagement and general wellbeing in cases of greater P-E fits (Kristof-Brown, Zimmerman, & Johnson, 2005), in scenarios of work environments having been radically transformed, as in the backdrop of this current COVID-19 crisis, a growing hiatus could sometimes lead to feelings of P-E misfits (Follmer, Talbot, Kristof-Brown, Astrove, & Billsberry, 2018).

HRM and the Implementation of Change

In the modern world, rather than material resources or physical assets, talent and knowledge are considered as the new foundations of wealth and the sources of competitive advantage. But to leverage on talent, organisations need to necessarily alter the way they strategise, organise and use human resources. More so during times of crisis and change.

The pandemic exhibited how some organisations can be swift and fast to reorient their HR strategies, processes and activities to meet such challenges of gigantic proportions. Many organisations took immediate steps to salvage the situation. Physical and mental health and employee wellbeing came into sharp focus as management agenda. BMC Software India Pvt. Ltd., which delivers software, services and know-how to help more than 10,000 customers, inclusive of 92% of the Forbes Global 100, started the #RemoteLife platform for employee engagement, comprising various contests, fun activities, sessions on mental well-being, tips on parenting, counselling on health care and the like, to facilitate cohesive work experience (BMC, Great Place to Work, 2020). Ericsson initiated a COVID-19 survey to gain insight into employee outlook, with the objective to ensure the well-being of employees as well as their family members (Ericsson, Great Place to Work, 2020). Salesforce.com, which is a customer relationship management company that brings organisations and customers together, launched the B-Well Together programme, a broadcast of half an hour, enunciating coping skills, guidelines and resources, from leading wellbeing experts and industry dignitaries such as Arianna Huffington, David Agus, Larry Brilliant, Deepak Chopra, Jack Kornfield, Plum Village Monastics and the like (Salesforce, Great Place to Work, 2020). CEAT started the Co-Fit 20 initiative, which is riveted on the physical as well as mental health of employees (CEAT, Great Place to Work, 2020). GE India undertook several interventions such as solving customised infrastructure needs at home or at the workplace, introducing personalised self-paced learning models, launching creative people engagement platforms and physical and mental well-being sessions and the like (GE, Great Place to Work, 2020). DHL Supply Chain India, the world's leading contract logistics provider, launched "Hello . . . Stay Connected" initiative, wherein all employees were dialled in by the HR team members, to ensure about the safety and well-being of the employees and their families (DHL, Great Place to Work, 2020). Ernst and Young, in order to safeguard the health and wellbeing of employees, started counselling support with trained psychologists and complementary doctor consultation for employees and their families (EY, Great Place to Work, 2020). Walmart India started online wellness sessions on physical fitness, mental health, financial literacy, parenting and family support, as a part of its new initiative christened 'Home is the New Workplace' (Walmart, Great Place to Work, 2020). HP enabled its Virtual Engagement platform, inclusive of Motivational Mondays, Learning Tuesdays, Wellness Wednesdays, Gratitude and giving Thursdays and Fun Fridays, to foster a sense of belongingness among the employees and to lighten their mood (HP, Great Place to Work, 2020). HIL Ltd., which is a flagship company of the $2.4 billion conglomerate CK Birla Group, offers comprehensive building materials and solutions for more than 70 years. In COVID times, HIL set up three cross-functional teams, namely "Code Blues", "The Snippeters" and "The Mavericks", to implement action plans around employee well-being and engagement. "Code Blues" is focused on employee health and safety, "The Snippeters" on effective communications and the "The Mavericks" on capability building and upskilling of employees (HIL, Great Place to Work, 2020).

Another area of focus was to keep the employees connected to their fellow colleagues, in a network of relationships, by devising new and innovative mechanisms of communication. InMobi Technology Services Pvt. Ltd., which works with the mission to power intelligent, mobile-first experiences for enterprises and consumers, undertook a multi-pronged initiative to support its employees, focusing on three broad tracks: well-being, collaboration and engagement and internal communication (InMobi, Great Place to Work, 2020). Altimetrik India Pvt. Ltd., which is an end-to-end business and technology transformation company, started a dedicated Facebook group, named "People of Altimetrik", for employees to share their work from home experiences (Altimetrik, Great Place to Work, 2020). Bajaj Finance launched a new initiative in this direction to reach out to each employee and addressed their concerns and issues of all sorts. They established a 24/7 helpline that employees and their family members can reach out to during crises (Bajaj Finance, Great Place to Work, 2020). Cadence, a leading provider of system design tools, software, IP and services, created a new online community, called the Work From Home Diaries, wherein employees can share fun and inspiring ideas, relating to cooking, exercising, carrying out home improvement projects, playing with kids, or anything outside of work, with the objective of spreading feelings of delight and companionship (Cadence, Great Place to Work, 2020).

This study is an attempt to examine the role the Human Resource Management function plays in originating and managing organisational change to bring in organisational success in variegated contexts. This book takes up specific instances of how organisations in their endeavours for growth and alignment have undergone the excruciating process of change and how the interplay of various subsystems in the company has facilitated such a change and the role of human resource management in the process of implementation of change.

A Discourse on Methodology

The objectives of this book have been examined through a qualitative case study research design. The authors scientifically investigate real-life phenomena within the environmental context and seek to bring out strands of patterns vis-à-vis the objectives set for the study. The authors take up six case studies on six distinct dimensions of the theme of the book. The multidimensionality, broadness, level and depth of the objectives of the book against the background of the complexities and volatility of the politico-social, economic, technological and legal environment propelled the authors to take up the case study method.

Not everything that can be counted counts and not everything that counts can be counted. Even as there may be controversy regarding who crafted this quote (Quote Investigator, 2021), it gives a very powerful message. Sometimes researchers feel the incessant need to reduce everything to quantifiable; however, this does not essentially make the best research strategy (Kaplan, 1964). Chabrol and Von Bertalanffy (1973) aver that the methods of classical science are inadequate in the case of interaction of a huge, albeit limited number of components.

Cases have been chosen because the cases are of inherent interest. Further, the cases are selected for theoretical reasons: for their propensity to offer insights into the phenomenon under enquiry. Theoretical sampling is considered appropriate for revealing and encompassing constructs and detecting relationships for the phenomena under investigation (Eisenhardt & Graebner, 2007).

The authors have examined several companies in their dimensions of organisational strategy and HR interventions, and Appendix 1 provides a list of such companies studied with respect to typology, the sector/industry it belongs to, the type of organisational change envisaged and the period of such change and the like. Based on the inherent value of the change dimension to be taken up, the authors have selected six companies from diverse backgrounds for in-depth analysis. Divergent dimensions of change have been taken up in each of the cases to facilitate the use of several perspectives for bringing about inferences from the different nuances of the study.

The dimensions studied vis-à-vis the cases are distinguishable in a significant manner with respect to the respective case. Thus, specific dimensions unique and specific to each company have been chosen for in-depth case study. Even as the book is an anthology of cases, it does not indulge in cross-case analysis, or in comparison of similarities and differences among cases, which is typical of multiple case study research. Instead, each case is analysed as a single case on its own, while exploring the opportunity to open a black box, by seeking to unravel deeper causes of the phenomenon within distinct contexts (Fiss, 2009). According to Dyer Jr and Wilkins (1991), case study research should prefer profound descriptions of individual cases, delve deep into the context and reveal insights emanating from the case and thereby contribute to theories. The comparison of multiple cases tends to indulge in superficial descriptions and weakens the possibility of context-related deep descriptions.

The case studies in this book have been undertaken against the backdrop of specific theoretical constructs exemplified by specific changing organisational strategy and the role of HR in the context of the implementation of specific transformational or change initiatives, either in a generic manner or vis-à-vis specific High-Performance Work Practices (HPWPs). These theoretical constructs have been delineated as a backdrop against each case in the Case Study chapter itself to present the cases as complete wholes.

Typical secondary source materials that have been collected include administrative proposals, progress reports, minutes of meetings, output of formal evaluations, board memoranda, inter-office memos and internal recommendations. The website information of respective organisations has also been referred to.

The primary data on all key areas of the case studies have been collected through semi-structured interviews. The interviews in this research have been generally guided by a schedule of open-ended questions. Interviews have been conducted with a range of managers and supervisors, CEOs and departmental heads of the respective organisations through interview schedules. Collated statistics regarding the number of interviews held and a specimen interview schedule are placed in Appendix 2 and Appendix 3, respectively, as a reference.

Data collected through interviews have been analysed using a constant comparative process of the main themes, as described by Glaser and Strauss (1967). Through comparative analysis, categories have been formed, boundaries of the categories have been delineated, segments have been assigned, contents have been summarised, similarities and discriminations have been established, patterns have been discovered and summaries have been concluded with respect to objectives set in each of the case studies. There has been no statistical analysis in these case studies, as the data collected have been essentially qualitative in nature.

The generalisability of each of the case studies is built on the strength of the description of the context of each case. Detailed descriptions regarding the background of the company would clearly exhibit the level of correspondence of these cases to similar other situations. The vision, mission and core values of the companies have also been spelled out to put things in perspective, as it is believed that the primary differentiator between successful companies and those which are not has been whether they have had developed a core ideology and an envisioned future or not (Mishra, Shukla, & Sujatha, 2019a). The financial parameters are collated in Appendix 4, even as other details such as organisational philosophy are elaborated in each case separately.

A Tour of the Book

The layout of the book is as under:

Introduction

Chapter 1 deals with an introduction that lays the foundation of the book by explaining elements of the book in brief. For this study, the introduction covers the objectives of the authors and how the authors have gone ahead with the identification of the Case Companies. It also presents the structure of the layout of the book.

Chapter 1: Global Efficiencies Through Local Practices

Blue Dart is South Asia's premier courier and integrated express package distribution company, which was taken over by DHL, a German multinational company. The case has been studied in the context of centralisation versus local adaptations and the role of Human Resource Management in adopting and implementing the best practices.

Chapter 2: Transformational Journey of an Indian 'Maharatna' Company

How does change come about? Is it an automated, unconscious process? Or is it a consciously manoeuvred process? In the incessant journey towards success and excellence, organisations at some stage or the other do their own soul-searching to pitchfork themselves in the trajectory to growth and expansion. What are the systems that inextricably interact to bring about change? Is Human Resource Management an essential function that must change its practices and processes to meet the requirements of organisational changes? This case study specifically examines the Organisational Transformation Exercise "Disha", both with respect to organisational and HR strategy, which was carried out in NTPC between 2002 and 2004 for its growth and expansion.

Chapter 3: Professionalisation of Family Business

Through the whirligig of time, quite often family businesses move toward increasing professionalisation. The role of the Human Resource Management function in adopting professional practices is studied in the context of Jindal Steel and Power Limited.

Chapter 4: Changing Contours of Unionism and HR as an Enabler

Participatory management is one of the HPWPs which many organisations are adopting. Changing contours of employee relations from collective bargaining to participative management and Trade Unions' adaptation to the same has quite often been facilitated by the adoption of robust HRM practices. This aspect has been studied in the case company of NALCO.

Chapter 5: HR's Strategic Interventions: A Study Against Miles and Snow's Typology

Miles and Snow (1978) build the paradigm of the Prospector-Analyzer-Defender-Reactor (P-A-D-R) strategy model of organisations. The role of HR in building support systems for fructification of the organisational strategy is studied in the context of L&T Electrical & Automation (E&A).

Chapter 6: Critical Success Factors in ERP-SAP Implementation and HR

In today's world, there is a demand for organisations to integrate all the business processes. Further, due to the disruptions brought about by technology, all segments of an organisation – viz. employees, internal and external customers and top management – are experiencing intense changes. All are experiencing what is technologically possible, and if something is possible, HR is expected to provide it. Odisha Power Generation Corporation has recently implemented SAP, which is an ERP solution. The present case study examines the relevance and importance of various critical success factors (CSFs) along the various stages of implementation of SAP.

Conclusions

The book is an attempt at demonstrating HR's role in organisation's change process through case study research. Such a role includes designing and implementing organisation development strategies, change interventions, or even functional level HPWPs. It involves developing training programs related to the change, assessing organisational readiness for change, developing timelines, communicating such strategies, building rewards systems to maintain and reinforce change, obtaining feedback from the employees during the change process in the organisation and supporting new behaviours to keep the firm competitive, and the like.

1 Global Efficiencies Through Local Practices

The entire gamut of social, cultural, economic, legal, institutional and political factors which make Indian business firmament a vortex of complexities proffers immense challenges to foreign companies right from the day of their initial entry to the Indian market to the execution of core functions. Such challenges range from significant inter-regional diversities within India to poor infrastructure and delays on account of systemic inefficiencies and corruption (Budhwar & Varma, 2011). This is true for the Human Resource Management function as well. Comparisons in terms of cross-cultural management show that India cannot be clustered into any of the formations of groups of nations because of its uniqueness (Sparrow & Budhwar, 1997), plummeting the potential for regional synergies.

Further, in view of the scarcity of literature on HRM in multinational companies (MNCs) in developing economies, strong variations in the internationalisation strategies among the emerging markets' MNCs (Sethi, 2009; Yaprak & Karademir, 2010), and the momentum in growth and change in many developing markets, the managerial systems of many MNCs are still evolving and are in a state of instability (Ghemawat & Hout, 2008).

Global Integration and Local Differentiation

In the past, there have been numerous deliberations regarding the management of multinational corporations with respect to their modes of entries into foreign markets, regulation, co-ordination, management of knowledge across subsidiaries and joint ventures (JVs) (Bartlett & Ghoshal, 1988), embracing of ethnocentric, polycentric or geocentric methods of structure of their Human Resource Management systems (Dowling, Festing, & Engles, 2008; Perlmutter, 1969; Tung & Lazarova, 2006; Zhu, 2019), global integration versus localisation of practices and multi-domestic or transnational structure and strategy (Bartlett & Ghoshal, 1988; Cela & Gatto, 2018; Paik & Sohn, 2004; Prahalad & Doz, 1987). A conglomerate of factors such

DOI: 10.4324/9781003191384-2

as context, company, local unit and International Human Resource Management policy working in unison influences the choice for an approach (Dowling et al., 2008). This results in global standardisation and localisation or 'glo-calisation' of HRM systems of MNCs.

The success of multinational corporations is ascribed to the efficacy of human resource management (HRM) (Bartlett & Ghoshal, 1995; Hosain, Arefin, & Hossin, 2020; Pucik, 1992). Several reasons may converge to propel multinational corporations to organise their Human Resource Management internationally and to transfer their parent practices to their subsidiaries abroad. If a firm has a positive experience with some specific Human Resource approaches, it may like to standardise them at the global level. Especially so, if it feels these are befitting to the local conditions (Dickmann & Muller-Camen, 2006). Vital reasons for this may be economies of scale, superior level of service delivery and better global synergy and efficiency (Bartlett & Ghoshal, 2002). Business practices that mirror core competencies and superior knowledge are assumed to be a source of competitive advantage (Bartlett & Ghoshal, 2002), and hence, MNCs would pursue to transplant their HRM practices, which have already been tested to be the right ones, into their operations in emerging economies (Beechler & Yang, 1994; Dowling & Welch, 2004; Hannon, Huang, & Jaw, 1995; Hetrick, 2002; Myloni, Harzing, & Mirza, 2004; Tayeb, 1998). Schuler, Sparrow, and Budhwar (2009) have contended that International HRM is critical for the success of MNCs, which often makes the difference between survival or extinction.

Kostova (1999) maintains that subsidiaries of MNC "may develop perceptions of dependence on the parent" due to various resources such as technology, capital and promotion of the subsidiary staff. She suggests that "under such conditions of dependency and intra-organizational competition", a subsidiary will seek to implement the parent company's practices as a method to gain internal legitimacy. Such resource dependence framework indicates that the greater the movement of various resources between the parent and the subsidiary, the stronger the MNC will exercise control over the Human Resource practices of the subsidiary (Kim & Mauborgne, 1993).

Brewster, Wood, and Brookes (2008) have observed that even though there is some indication of common global Human Resource practices among MNCs, enough diversity in practices persists, which could be explained by the persistent effects of institutional realities. Cultural, cognitive and normative institutional practices enveloping in the background of the host country play significant parts in the HRM practices in conditions of uncertainty (DiMaggio & Powell, 1983; Levitt & March, 1988). While the institutional theory has been widely used in the study of MNCs, Kostova, Roth, and Dacin (2008) propose that there lurks a hazard of an "implied institutional imperialism" in the Western interpretation of the role of MNCs, and, hence, they suggest broadening the theoretical paradigm on adopting a "blended institutional perspective, where the broad concepts of social embeddedness of organisations are intertwined with the ideas of agency, social construction, power and politics" (p. 1003).

Edwards (2004) observes that "employees, as actors at various levels of plant may be reluctant to share their knowledge, expertise with their counter parts expatriate employees, for fear of undermining their performance within the group". This could lead to organisational politics which could play a pivotal role in what and how much of multinational cultural practices could transfer from the parent company to subsidiaries.

When a JV or subsidiary is largely entrenched in a home-grown setup, its Human Resource practices are greatly tampered with by local forces (Rosenzweig & Nohria, 1994; Wright & McMahan, 1992). It has been reported (Braun & Warner, 2002) that the HRM practices in organisations in which the MNC holds a minority share are more locally adjusted than those in foreign completely owned and majority-owned units. Farley, Hoenig, and Yang (2004) observe numerous important alterations in HRM practices between foreign subsidiaries and JV s. The background and profile of the HR manager are expected to influence the effects of isomorphic pulls. An HR manager recruited from a local organisation is more likely to identify native companies as the referent point and this is likely to affect the type of initiatives advocated and executed in the unit (Bjorkman & Lu, 2001; Shenkar & Zeira, 1987).

Dicken (1994) describes the business processes as a blend of intra- and inter-firm structures of relationships, designed by dissimilar grades and forms of power and effect over inputs, throughputs and outputs. The survival of a multinational corporation in a host country, thus, rests on its flexibility to adapt to the established national culture and simultaneously striving to attain the strategic goals for the parent MNCs as "networks of alliances" that criss-crosses the national boundaries and industrial sectors (Lorange & Johan, 1993).

In emerging economies like China and India, even as there exists a big group of local labour, the abilities and competencies required for employability as international standards are still lacking (Budhwar & Varma, 2011; Ready, Hill, & Conger, 2008). At the same time bringing in expatriates in large numbers is both costly and unviable. Ready et al. (2008) contend firms have no alternative but to cultivate local talent. In such a scenario, initially Rosenzweig and Nohria (1994) and later Ryan and Gibbons (2011) trust that the shifting global occupational trends are drawing MNCs more towards local sensitivities or isomorphism than towards global integration.

MNC's subsidiaries and JVs are perceived as tampered both with institutional factors in the host country and with global isomorphic processes, such as downward spiral of pressures from the MNC's parent company (Westney, 1993). The management of human resources in a multinational corporation is influenced by several contextual factors, such as the country of origin (Harzing & Sorge, 2003), corporate strategy (Bartlett & Ghoshal, 2002), International HRM strategy (Taylor, Beechler, & Napier, 1996), business structure (Ulrich, Younger, & Brockbank, 2008), International HRM structure (Farndale et al., 2010), CEO perceptions (Brandl & Pohler, 2010; Chung, Bozkurt, & Sparrow, 2012) and cross-cultural issues (Gupta & Bhaskar, 2016).

Researchers have demonstrated that there exist several obstacles to the success of the transfer of international practices to host countries; some pertain to the features of the initiatives being transferred and others to the cultural mores and organisational contexts (Ghoshal & Bartlett, 1988; Szulanski, 1996; Zander & Kogut, 1999). Some contend that regional-level policies, laws and institutional factors, mediate the push of globalisation and form responses at the national level, and hence, it may be likely that regionalisation will affect convergence between firms originating from the same region, but divergence inter-regionally (John & Chattopadhyay, 2020).

Kostova (1999) suggests that the fruitfulness of international transference of organisational processes is intermediated by the equivalence between three different sets of factors, relating to the social, organisational and relational contexts. The social context is the institutional remoteness between the geographies of the company in the country of origin and the host country. The organisational context is the organisational culture of the host country. And the relational context is the background of relationships between the parent company and the recipient unit. Kovach, R.C. (1994) and Kovach, K.A. (1995) also highlight the problems involved in the transference of practices to different subsidiaries worldwide because of the perceptual divergences among employees of dissimilar nationalities.

To resolve such issues, MNCs and their JVs and subsidiaries should seek an equilibrium between the execution of HRM practices that conform to the reasonable expectations and necessities of the host country and the pursuit of more distinguishing practices in their country of origin (Gunnigle, Murphy, Cleveland, Heraty, & Morley, 2001). To face realistic challenges, MNCs do have the best approaches from both HQ and host country culture (Doeringer, Lorenz, & Terkla, 2003).

Whether new ideas and innovation are pursued to be developed within each host country subsidiary or pursued to be cascaded down to the entire network of the MNC by the parent company would depend on the context and situation of each case. Many modern MNCs, therefore, need to choose a transnational strategy, to master both the art of cost reduction and local differentiation for maintaining a competitive edge (Bartlett & Ghoshal, 2002).

The role of parent organisation would be to effectually draw the lines of demarcation between degrees of centralisation and control and the degrees of decentralisation and autonomy while deciding whether to allow the subsidiary units to take independent decisions in response to the local demands enforced by its native context (Doz & Prahalad, 1984).

Blue Dart: Company Background of a German Multinational's Indian Acquisition

Couriers have been around for several years. The earliest of the couriers were runners and horseback riders, who delivered messages. These were the days before the advent of mechanised transportation, so foot messengers ran for kilometres to reach their destinations. Organised courier industry started in India in 1979 as DHL Worldwide Express entered the Indian market through a contract with Airfreight Ltd. ONGC was the first Indian corporate house which used their express services.

Blue Dart Express Limited is a leading express company in India. It was established as 'Blue Dart Courier Services' in 1983. Towards the end of 2004, DHL India, a multinational Logistics Service Provider (LSP) company, acquired a 68 per cent equity in Blue Dart. Blue Dart eventually evolved into being the largest third-party logistics service provider for most of the leading industry segments in India.

Third-party logistics (3PL) implies outsourcing transportation, warehousing and other logistics-related activities that were originally performed in-house, to a 3PL service provider. The outsourcing part is now converted into fully integrated logistics solutions and is taken care of by Logistics Service Providers (LSPs) which provide multiple benefits of cost reduction, in-time delivery and improved efficiency of the supply chain. Third-Party Logistics providers (3PLs) are also referred to as logistics outsourcing or contract logistics. However, this service these companies provide is more than just outsourcing or subcontracting (Marasco, 2008). Typically, outsourcing or subcontracting deals with a single product or for a single function, or with a single vendor. However, 3PLs provide manifold logistics services for multiple products to multiple vendors concurrently (Wee Kwan Tan, Yifei, Zhang, & Hilmola, 2014).

3PL is defined as "the use of external companies to perform logistics functions that have traditionally being performed within an organization" (Lieb, 1992). LSPs are "Companies which perform logistics activities on behalf of others" as averred by Delfmann, Albers, and Gehring (2002).

Stretching open the rolled-up scrolls of history, one would see the concept of logistics outsourcing originated during the Middle Ages. In Europe, the origins of several LSPs can be traced to the Middle Ages (Lynch, 2002). Outlining the evolution of logistics outsourcing during recent times, it is found that, in the 1950s and 1960s, logistics outsourcing was limited to transportation and warehousing. The transactions were mainly short-term. In the 1970s, the importance was attached to improved productivity, cost reduction and long-term contracts, while value-added services such as packaging, labelling, systems support and inventory management were proffered in the 1980s. Since the 1990s, outsourcing has gained momentum, and more value-added services are being provided. Some of them are import/export supervision, customs authorisation, freight forwarding, customer service, rate negotiation, order processing, assembly/installation, distribution, order fulfilment, reverse logistics, consulting services that include distribution network planning, site selection for facility location, fleet management, freight consolidation, logistics audit, etc.

The services of Logistics Service Providers are extended from transportation and warehousing into integrated logistics solutions in the form of one-stop destination for all shopping (Kumar & Singh, 2012). Now, logistics service providers perform multiple functions such as bulk procurement, inbound and outbound transportation, order processing, warehousing, fleet management, shipment consolidation, distribution network optimisation, value-added services and speedy on-time delivery to the end-users (Kumar & Singh, 2012). Sahay and Mohan (2006) found that the common logistics services in India are inbound and outbound transportation, warehousing activities, order fulfilment and fleet management.

Supply chain integration is an important component for the growing efficacy and lucrativeness of LSPs is discussed by many researchers (Kumar & Singh, 2012). Decreasing margins and a harsher competitive milieu together constitute the main driving force for the growth of 3PL. Flexibility in service (Naim, Aryee, & Potter, 2010) and optimal delivery time (Ulku & Bookbinder, 2012) are also found most frequently used in outsourced logistics functions. There have been studies on the latest logistics practices like green supply chain and reverse logistics (Govindan, Palaniappan, Zhu, & Kannan, 2012). Many best practices followed by LSPs, such as channel partnering, route optimisation, supply chain integration, environment friendliness, that is, green and reverse logistics, IT innovations, resource optimisation and flexibility in service, are the reasons for large-scale adoption of services of LSPs.

Blue Dart is the premier courier and integrated express package distribution company in South Asia. It carries out door-to-door pickup and delivery of packages, documents and shipments in India and throughout the world. It was created as 'Blue Dart Courier Services' in 1983 by three entrepreneurs. Its promoters were Mr Clyde Cooper, Mr Kushroo Dubash and Mr Tushar Jani. It was incorporated as a private limited company in 1991 and was transformed into a public limited company in September 1994. Its emergence heralded the birth of the systematised express industry in India.

The company entered into business arrangements with Gelco International (UK) in 1983, which was acquired by Federal Express (FedEx), a world leader in the express industry, in 1984. Blue Dart continued as a global service participant of FedEx till 2002, when it entered into a contract with DHL, another global player in the international express market.

Later, towards the end of 2004, DHL India acquired 68 per cent equity in Blue Dart by purchasing equity from the promoters and by making an open offer in the market. DHL Express (Singapore) Pte. Ltd. completed the purchase of 81.03% of the equity capital of Blue Dart Express Limited in 2005 even as the company continued as an independent identity from DHL India. Mr. Clyde Cooper was retained as a director.

Blue Dart has the most widespread domestic network encompassing over 34,267 sites and services more than 220 countries and territories at the global plane through its group company DHL. Its vision is "to establish continuing excellence in delivery capabilities focused on the individual customer" (Blue Dart, 2021). It operates through diverse modes of transport – both surface and air.

Blue Dart has been continuously growing in revenue over the last ten-year period. In Jan-Dec 2006 its total income stood at Rs. 669.76 crores and from April 2019 to March 2019 at Rs. 3,184.00 crores. During the period, the profit after tax has grown from Rs. 50.23 crores to Rs. 88.00 crores. The year-wise total income of Blue Dart since 2006 and the year-wise profit after-tax numbers of Blue Dart are depicted in Appendix 4.

Some salient points of Blue Dart's business and e-strategy are required to be delineated here to put things in perspective. Needless to mention that customer focus and large-scale usage of technology have been the mainstay of Blue Dart, which ensure its leadership position in the industry.

Its service via Air Mode is christened "Domestic Priority 1030", which is

> a guaranteed door-to-door time-definite delivery of shipments by air the next possible business day by 10:30 hours, targeted at time-critical business-to-business needs . . . an Express time definite service with Money Back Guarantee (MBG) to the select pin codes in Chennai, Delhi, Ahmedabad, Mumbai, Hyderabad, Bangalore, Navi Mumbai and Gurgaon by 10:30 hrs on the next possible business day.
>
> (Blue Dart, 2021)

'Domestic Priority 1030' is operated via Blue Darts' own flights for the major metros of India and these further are connected to diverse other locations either by domestic flights or by trains.

To serve large items of low importance, Blue Dart possesses a fleet of over 9,400 vehicles and offers a complete solution through surface mode in the form of 'Dart Surface Line'. Dart Surfaceline is an inexpensive, door-to-door, ground delivery service to over 35,008 locations in India for consignments weighing 10 kg and above. It offers a cost-effective logistics option for less time-sensitive deliveries, with various value-added features and benefits such as Time-bound Delivery, Cash on Delivery, Demand Draft on Delivery, Freight on Delivery, Insurance Arrangement, Regulatory Clearances and Pick-up Convenience, etc.

Blue Dart has been the forerunner in providing a multimodal system of transport by providing a mix of air and surface. This service christened 'Dart Apex' was initiated in 1994. Dart Apex is a door-to-door, time-bound delivery service within India for consignments weighing 10 kg and above. It is a fast, efficacious distribution solution for commercial consignments that are required to undergo regulatory clearances or require special handling and yet are to be delivered within a defined timeframe. Under Dart Apex, load from locations not connected by air is sent by surface mode to the nearest centre being serviced by Blue Dart Aviation. From there, it is forwarded to other major metros, from where again it is connected by surface mode to the place of delivery.

As a leader in technology solutions in the industry of supply-chain management in India, Blue Dart Express Limited has developed an e-strategy. This e-strategy "encompasses E-Solutions to deliver additional process efficiencies to business by allowing them access to Blue Dart's e-shipping tools and integration with its e-business tools" (Blue Dart, 2021).

Blue Dart was the first to establish a state-of-the-art track and trace system COSMAT-I in 1991. Currently, it is using COSMAT-II, an acronym for Computerised On-line System for Management, Accounting and Tracking, which is a complete ERP system developed by Blue Dart in-house. It interfaces with the various in-house management systems to give real-time, thorough and precise information about the customers' consignments. COSMAT II was created in four major modules to cover multifarious processes of the whole organisation. Now consignments are scanned from pick-up to all the transit points till delivery, by means of bar coding and laser scanner technology, diffusing updates automatically to its Oracle database. COSMAT II enables easy access to the database over a wide area network and guarantees dependable information and response. COSMAT II is an evolving system, upgraded unceasingly, to provide value to the customer and make processes easier, secure and controllable.

Tracking of the shipment through the system is also allowed through TrackDart, by using the TrackDart box. Waybill Number or the reference number can be used to track the status of shipments through MailDart Through Location Finder, customers can find the service whereabouts of Blue Dart and the Blue Dart counter or franchisee located nearest to them. Similarly, prospective customers can prognosticate the possible transit time and price by using Transit Time Finder and Price Finder.

SMART, an acronym for Space Management Allocation Reservations and Tracking system, has been developed in the year 1995, for its aircraft. This is the first cargo management system in the country for real-time space and revenue management on the Blue Dart Aviation network. SMART merges into COSMAT II which guarantees that packages taken through SMART are lifted, relocated on the network and followed until delivery.

Blue Dart's online system for customer complaint-redressal, CARESS, allows intelligence on each customer grievance and helps enhance fineness in service delivery. It is an acronym for Complaint Appreciation, Resolution and Evaluation to Satisfaction System.

The Human Resource System

HR Structure

The HR department has a two-tier structure in the organisation:

Corporate Level

Corporate HR has direct reporting to MD. Corporate HR has five verticals, being handled by five direct reports, who take care of Training & Development, HR Operations, Recruitment, Talent Management, Compensation & Benefits and Employee relations.

Regional Level

There are six regions, each having a Regional HR Manager, who has a matrix reporting to the Head HR and administrative reporting to the regional head. Each of these RHRMs has separate verticals of HR in the regions.

HR Function

The Human Resource (HR) function is a strategic business partner at Blue Dart. Head HR is represented in the executive committee of the company. The HR function is aligned with the organisational business by the adoption of a two-level strategy.

HR formulates both short- and long-term HR strategies in line with the company goals, strategy and plans. The key people agenda gets incorporated in the corporate objectives as part of HR Objectives. In line with the best practices in the industry, HR has played a significant role in formulating and implementing employee-friendly and business-related policies and practices. Some of the key initiatives are as under:

At Blue Dart, there is a robust Human Resource Information System (HRIS) called People Related Information systems for Development & Empowerment (PRIDE) module, which is a PeopleSoft HRMS. It is an online self-service evaluation management application for leaders, managers, employees and human resources (HR) administrators. It takes care of all the key employee-related activities. E-performance supports the entire planning and evaluation process, from planning and aligning employee performance to creating developmental goals with enterprise objectives, through assessing and rewarding employee performance results along with the assessment of right behaviour.

The company has taken several measures for developing talent in Blue Dart, which is given herewith.

Succession Planning

All the first-line employees and their successors are mapped to their relevant competencies and their competencies are evaluated and reviewed from time to time. Further, the career path of the employees is framed on the basis of the various grades so that along with the organisation's benefit, the individual employees' career aspirations are also taken into consideration.

Management Trainee (MT) and GET (Graduate Executive Trainee) Program

Blue Dart has started the management trainee program to encourage the inflow of new ideas and to create a leadership pipeline with the induction of new talent. An effective mentoring program is also in place to mentor and coach the Trainees in their training phase and even after that. Graduate Executive Training (GET), called 'Umang', is a frontline operational leadership development program at Blue Dart. It is a career development initiative for nurturing young talents and grooming the GETs to become future leaders of Blue Dart Express Limited.

Learning and Development

As per the philosophy of the company "Blue Dart is a learning organization and encourages development of knowledge, skills and attitudes to enable its people to perform to their full potential" (Blue Dart, 2021). It has established a company-wide training set-up and brings learning opportunities to the workplace by deploying both in-house qualified trainers as well as by implementing e-learning initiatives through the Intranet. Training need analysis is carried out at the individual level, developmental objectives are set and suitable modules are implemented. Further, the effectiveness of the training is evaluated by using the training Management Information System (MIS).

Internal Growth Opportunities at Blue Dart

Since its inception, the HR at Blue Dart has been following a strategy of grooming and growing frontline personnel through planned exposure, rotation, developmental input and by providing career opportunities to the frontline staff as part of its career development policy. All key roles are filled up through internal managers to the extent possible, and in case a skillset is not available within the company, talent is hired from outside. The majority of the leadership roles, that is, Managing Director, Finance Director and Chief Operating Officer, Customer Service Head, Air OPS Head, all Regional and Sales Heads and IT heads have grown internally.

Employee Satisfaction Survey

Started in 1992, the Employee Satisfaction Survey (ESS) process in Blue Dart has been regarded as an unheard-of initiative in the service sector for its time. Since then it is one of the most important annual exercises for the organisation. Consistently, the participation percentage of 98% for the last couple of years is a testimony to the bonding amongst employees. Blue Dart has been achieving high overall mean satisfaction scores consistently for years. The questionnaire consists of dimensions like Rewards, Job Condition, Leadership (Corporate and Units), New Initiatives, Employee Engagement, etc. Through inputs from the ESS feedback sessions with the employees, many of the policies/interventions have been implemented, such as an increase in staff advance amount, increase in the level of availing compensatory off to middle managers (which was earlier limited only till junior managers earlier), etc. Organisational health with key parameters like

Active Leadership and Employee engagement is measured through the ESS process. ESS process reflects pride for working in Blue Dart as one of the highest-ranking values with more than 96% score.

The ESS survey in 2016 was conducted with a planned approach focused on facilitating senior management interaction with employees and clarification sessions on ESS issues/employee touch points. Pride for Working in Blue Dart' had a score of 97.4% and 'My future in Blue Dart' scored 95.6%. Employee engagement also emerged as one of the highest-scoring items with a score of 94.8%. A few other parameters such as 'Job secured with good performance', 'Blue Dart does a good job for customers' and 'Working in Blue Dart is good for me', also returned high scores.

Grievance Redressal Policy

Blue Dart's Grievance Redressal Policy ensures that employee grievances are addressed. If unresolved, it is taken at the highest management levels of the organisation.

As the forgoing explains, after taking over by DLF, Blue Dart continues to be governed more by local adaption than through global integration. However, some of the best practices have been directly cascaded down from DHL. Some of these are explained herewith.

Employee of the Year Awards

This global award is presented by the parent group, DHL, and is the most prestigious award at Blue Dart. Employee of the Year (EOY) is the highest award recognised by the DPDHL group and this is awarded to employees up to the manager's level. This is given on the basis of the outstanding and extra mile work in the area of customer satisfaction, process excellence, revenue generation, cost savings and optimisation and in respect of any such other project which may lead to business gains. This award is the biggest honour that is bestowed upon an employee for an extraordinary contribution having a positive impact on the organisation on a wide scale. The employee selected for this recognition is given 3–4 days of company-sponsored trip to a location outside India where she attends the EOY Award function, and the award is given by the CEO of the Business Divisions. Also, the awardee is given a cash prize of Euro 500, a memento and a certificate.

Other Awards

To motivate the employees and recognise good work and extra mile contributions, Blue Dart has instituted many other rewards and recognitions. Some of the prominent awards include Bravo Blue Darter and Super Darter. These recognitions have had been followed for a long time, even before Blue Dart becoming a part of DHL. Bravo Blue Darter award is given to any employee for doing some outstanding work for customer service or process improvement etc. This is an on-the-spot award. The awardee is a given a Bravo Blue Darter Memento, a certificate and Rs. 500 as a cash award. An employee can receive this award as many times as one is selected and the decision for the award is taken by her manager.

Motiv8 Framework

The performance management system in Blue Dart for all management cadre employees is managed through the online HRIS platform, PRIDE, known as Motiv8 ePMS. Blue Dart follows Key Result Area (KRA) and Competency-based framework of ePMS. It has a subset of eight competencies, known as Motiv8, which drives the competency framework and is used to assess the potential of employees at various levels.

Panel Review

This is a succession planning initiative being conducted at Blue Dart, which has been launched in 2011. This is an initiative comprising 360-degree reviews for identifying high potential employees. This comprises a panel discussion regarding the development of employees carried out by a cross-functional team consisting of the regional heads, functional heads and Managing Director (for first line potential successors). The Panel Discussion is followed by a feedback session and finalisation of an Individual Development Plan (IDP).

Appreciation Fortnight

Blue Dart is known for its employee passion and commitment. Although this culture of appreciation pervades almost all fora, it was felt that if there is a structured platform and appreciation is formalised during a specific period, it would encourage employees to appreciate each other and would act as a more powerful tool for achieving the corporate objective. In an endeavour to make this happen, thanksgiving and appreciation have been formalised as a structured process. The first-ever Appreciation Week in Blue Dart was formally launched on 9 November 2015, and it went on till 21 November 2015. The second edition, Appreciation Fortnight was celebrated from 9 to 21 November 2016.

PeP Certification Training

Group strategy 2020's Connect pillar emphasises the importance of "Certified specialists for everything we do!" to achieve quality leadership and service excellence. Hence, HR has created a customised certified Programme for Post-eCommerce-Parcel (Pep) Department called PeP Expert. Pep certified training is an initiative of the group to develop a can-do attitude for driving change and the future growth of the organisation. This is a top-down OD intervention and the training is facilitated by internal managers trained as facilitators. All employees are to be covered in this programme by the end of 2020. Blue Dart has started this journey in 2016.

Upstairs 2016

Drawing from the Deutsche Post DHL Group's corporate responsibility strategy, UPstairs – GoTeach Initiative has been implemented to promote equal educational opportunities. Through the Upstairs program, the company supports the employees' children with financial assistance.

Blue Dart Case: Concluding Observations

Even after the acquisition by DHL, Blue Dart Express Limited continues as an independent identity from DHL India. This demonstrates that even though the company has leveraged the global support systems of DHL, it continues with the robust business practices prevalent in the local conditions. It is also evident from the case that Blue Dart is an ideal example of a multinational company where global efficiencies are achieved largely through local practices (Mishra, Shukla, & Sujatha, 2018). Duly supported by HR, it has built its leadership pipeline through home-grown talent for which majority of the leadership roles in Blue Dart India, that is, Managing Director, Finance Director, Chief Operating Officer, Customer Service Head, Air OPS Head, all Regional and Sales Heads and IT heads have grown internally through the ranks of Blue Dart India. In HR, the policies, systems and practices of Blue Dart are primarily India-centric catering to the local requirements. However, the best practices prevalent in DHL at the global level such as the Employee of the Year (EOY) award, certification as specialists Programme and Motiv8 framework, etc. are adopted in India.

2 Transformational Journey of an Indian 'Maharatna' Company

Firms are said to be successful when the products they produce or the service they provide have a steady demand in the market and there is cost optimisation, so a steady profit is generated (Doz & Hamel, 1998). For the attainment of this goal, companies do focus on devising their systems and processes aligned to such goals and devise their "winning formula" for success. Winning formulae necessitates that supporting competencies are ingrained in each component of the firm's value chain (Tregoe & Zimmerman, 1982; Veliu & Manxhari, 2017). When an organisation's winning formula gets accepted and established, the organisation takes up a unique identity that defines its vision, mission and values as well as its short and long-term goals intentions and priorities (Weick, 1993) which further leads to employees' individual goal internalisation and successful pursuit of the same (Gagné, 2018). However, winning formulae are never permanent and do get obsolete when they become out of synch with the changing times. When this happens, the organisation requires a radical transformation so that its strategy, systems and processes are re-aligned with the ribs of new realities.

Strategising in a Public Sector

Insanity is repeating the same mistakes but expecting different results. In order to get over the vicious circle of mediocrity and underperformance, organisations need to make appropriate strategic choices zooming in on the critical issues that drive company performance. Strategy is the collective pattern an organisation displays and operationalises to ensure its development and growth, by positioning itself in unique ways to create and add stakeholder value. The strategy explains how an organisation intends to move forward and how it positions itself to safeguard the interests of its stakeholders. An effective strategy reflects the raison d'etre of the organisation, elucidates strategic choices and differentiating and inimitable positions, gives clarity on the different systems and processes for value creation,

DOI: 10.4324/9781003191384-3

implements suitable metrics for measuring progress and brings about congruence between the organisation and stakeholders' interests (Magretta, 2011; Montgomery, 2012; Porter, 1996). Strategy is a multidimensional concept, with ingredients drawn on both internal and external milieu. It represents a system of value creation with mutually reinforcing components (Magretta, 2011; Montgomery, 2012).

Strategising, or organisational strategy development and execution, is a process of thinking and learning and building logic for producing sustainable value, and therefore, forms the bedrock on which the whole edifice of an organisation's competitive potential rests in a specific context. Strategising is the process through which leaders of organisations "show the way" (Spears, 2010), envision the future and carve out a conceivable way forward towards it. As confirmed in a 2015 survey (Rigby & Bilodea, 2015), strategic planning is one of the most used business tools across the world.

Strategy formulation as a process in the public sector is pretty like the ones in the private sector (Joyce, 2004). Even as strategising has become pervasive in the public sector over the past few decades, strategic planning in the Public sector needs to involve management of the organisation's overarchic strategic agenda on a continuing, rather than in a sporadic manner (Poister, 2010).

Quite often studies in strategic management, including the ones on the Public sector, do not provide details of strategising practices (Hoglund, 2015; Jarzabkowski & Kaplan, 2015). However, the value lies in the understanding of a micro perspective of strategy and thus strategising consists in the "planning, resource allocation, monitoring and control practices and processes through which strategy is enacted" (Jarzabkowski & Fenton, 2006). In this context, in-depth case studies become a necessity for understanding the strategy and strategising perspective (Melin, Johnson, & Whittington, 2003), and the extant case study is an attempt in that direction.

NTPC: The Largest Power-Generating Company in India

In 1975, the National Thermal Power Corporation Limited (NTPC) was formed with the objective of planning, promoting and organising integrated development of thermal power (including Associated Transmission Systems) in the country.

NTPC commissioned its first unit at Singrauli in February 1982. Today, it is India's largest State-owned power company. Now it is one of the four Maharatna Companies in the country and is ranked No. 2 Independent Power Producer (IPP) in Platts Top 250 Global Energy Company rankings. The total installed capacity of NTPC is 66,900 MW (including Joint

Ventures). NTPC owns 24 coal-based, seven gas-based, one Hydro, one Wind, 13 Solar and one Small hydro plant. Under Joint Ventures, NTPC has nine coal-based, four gas-based and 13 renewable energy projects.

The vision statement of NTPC is "To Be the World's Leading Power Company, Energizing India's Growth". Its mission statement is to "Provide Reliable Power and Related Solutions in an Economical, Efficient and Environment-Friendly Manner, Driven by Innovation and Agility". Its core values stand for "ICOMIT" or integrity, Customer Focus, Organisational Pride, Mutual Respect & Trust, Innovation and Learning and Total Quality and Safety.

The operating performance of NTPC has been noticeably above the national average. During the fiscal year 2019–2020, the PLF of NTPC coal stations was 68.20% as compared to all India PLF of 58.08%. Over the years, NTPC has consistently operated at much higher operating efficiency as compared to All India operating performance. As on 31 March 2020, NTPC had 16.78% of the total national capacity and, it contributes 20.96% of the total power generation of the country, which is achieved due to the overall thrust on operational efficiency.

Financial Performance

The total revenue, profit after tax and value-added per employee over more than a decade are depicted in Appendix 4. These figures show that value-added per employee has consistently increased over the years and this speaks highly of HR's strategy of augmenting the competency and productivity of the employees.

Organisational Transformation Exercise 'Disha'

In the incessant journey towards success and excellence, organisations often do their own soul-searching for strategy formulations to lift themselves in the trajectory of growth and expansion. NTPC Limited similarly did its own soul-searching in 2002 through 2005 with the objective of becoming a world-class power utility. It launched a comprehensive organisational transformation exercise named Project Disha in January 2002. It retained international consultants A. T. Kearney to assist it in this transformation exercise. The entire exercise was divided into two phases, as described herewith:

Diagnostic Phase

During the initial few months, a comprehensive diagnostic study was initiated. This exercise aimed to review the extant situation of NTPC and identify the key issues and challenges facing NTPC. The diagnostic exercise also identified the initiatives that were required to be taken up to achieve the objectives of Project Disha.

Design Phase

The initiatives identified during Diagnostic Phase were taken up for detailed design. Various options for each of the initiatives were developed and evaluated by the team. These analyses were exhaustively discussed with functional departments, cross-functional teams, and various senior management resources prior to recommending suitable options.

The objective of the present study is to explore how the top-down, voluntary transformational exercise was carried out and implemented in NTPC and helped it pitchfork itself to the position of one of the top four Maharatna Companies in India. This case study examines the strategic transformational exercise recommended for and implemented by NTPC and simultaneously examines the change initiatives recommended for and implemented in HR strategy and explores and describes associations between the two.

The Sixteenth Electric Power Survey published by the Central Electricity Authority in September 2000, projected energy demand of about 975.22 billion units by the end of the 11th plan period and about 1,318.64 billion units by the end of the 12th plan period. In effect, this would call for a trebling of energy generation over the next 15 years.

While several policy initiatives had been taken up during the 1990s, private participation in the sector had not increased as envisaged. This had resulted in increased dependence on state and central utilities to meet the capacity addition targets. However, the financial position of the state utilities was challenged and the onus of adding to the generation capacity in line with demand rested largely on NTPC, which was the largest power generating company and a key player in the power sector.

This changing business firmament presented several opportunities to NTPC for growth: viz. expand generation capacities by putting up thermal and hydro capacities; broad base fuel mix by considering imported coal, gas, domestic coal, nuclear power, etc. with a view to mitigate fuel risks and maintain long-run competitiveness; lead the development and commercial deployment of non-conventional energy sources, especially in the distributed generation mode; expand services for Engineering, Procurement and Construction (EPC), Renovation and Modernisation (R&M) and Operation and Maintenance (O&M) activities in both the domestic and international markets; backward integrate into fuel management to exercise greater control and understanding of supply economics; improve collections by trading and direct sale to bulk customers; execute increased number of power plants that classify for Mega Power Project status, thereby reducing the cost of projects and power generated; and forward integrate into the distribution business in India, and the like.

Disha: On Organisational Strategy and HRM

Disha gave its recommendations on divergent aspects of company strategy, as detailed herewith:

Business Strategy

For the growth to be beneficial to its value, NTPC needed to adopt a balanced perspective integrating both top-line and bottom-line growth objectives, which should also address the aspirations of the employees of NTPC and provide adequate opportunities for NTPC to build on their competencies. Some of the key recommendations were to focus more on customers through institutionalising a process for tracking customer health, strengthening customer interfaces and assisting in customer reform, adopt a proactive regulatory management process so as to better align with the regulator and mitigate regulatory risk, align the strategy to the various availability and pricing scenarios for different fuel options, consider diversifying businesses to include coal mining, coal washeries, distribution and hydro-based generation and establish a global footprint through engineering and operations related services in Asia Pacific, Middle East and African markets.

Business Process Reengineering and IT

Key processes in all the functions were reviewed. While acknowledging that since its establishment, NTPC has had been demonstrating an elevated level of performance, to achieve a considerable reduction in the project completion time and at the same time having high availability levels which were comparable with international utilities, it proposed a system that would require an integrated IT system for its successful implementation, as it would have to draw information from multiple departments like Materials, Operation and Maintenance (O&M), etc.

Restructuring

Recommendations for restructuring of the organisation were made with a view to bring in coordinated structure for project planning and execution, adequate empowerment for efficient plant operations, structured approach to strategic planning, the focus of Board on strategic issues of growth and diversification and realigned regional structure for organisational flexibility.

Disha also helped identify structural interventions opportunities for NTPC: viz. optimal structure for management of Fuel Diversification (Hydro Projects); optimal structure for management of Business Diversification (Coal Mining, Distribution, etc.); strategic focus to IT; establishing greater customer support and regulatory interface systems within NTPC; restructuring Board sub-committees; redefining the scope of Management Committees and recommending suitable changes in Delegation of Powers to support restructured business processes and decision-making, etc.

Human Resource Strategy was to form a very important segment on which the entire organisational transformation strategy was to rivet. Disha's Design recommendations regarding HR strategy were to build on the already existing paradigm of NTPC's current HR strategy of Competence building, Commitment building, Culture building and Systems Building and bring in new interventions within the ambit of this overall HR strategy.

Building Competency

Here, Disha recommended continuation of the existing interventions: viz. imparting training mandatorily for 7 days to all employees; structuring of the training and development programs in technical and functional competencies based on the gaps emanating from the outcome of performance evaluation process, Development Centre Feedback, individual developmental plans and organisational requirements; two-pronged training strategy based on Need-based training and Planned Interventions; educational programs, such as M. Tech in Power Generation (for Executives) through IIT Delhi and Bachelor of Science program (for Diploma engineers) through BITs, Pilani; advanced training programs, e.g. Advanced Management Programs (AMP) for leadership; developing global competencies by way of foreign training; exposure to world-class practices in technology, innovation, Research and Development (R&D) practices and best practices in Power business, developmental initiatives through job rotation, career paths and development centres, strengthening of succession-planning process for all senior-level positions, knowledge-sharing initiatives such as Professional Circles and NTPC Open Competition for Executive Talent.

Further, under the gamut of building competencies, Disha recommended a few new initiatives; viz. creation of the Managerial and Technical/functional Competency Directories, which were envisaged to be the central reference database for critical HR processes in the organisation like recruitment, performance management, career development, training and rewards; piloting of a competency assessment programme and highlighting the required training interventions emanating out of it; and preparation of a Key Performance Areas (KPA) directory which was to be used as a reference directory to identify KPAs, weightages and measures of performance applicable to various roles and functions and the like.

Disha recommended that leadership succession criteria may be defined for leadership positions up to two levels below the board, which should form the basis for developing and selecting successors. Even as talent-hiring would continue to be done at the induction level for infusing fresh minds for continuous renewal and strengthening the Manpower pool of the company, considering the business diversifications and new business plans in mind, the key talents with the required experience, skill, competency and exposure profile not available in the company, but essential for driving the new businesses shall be hired from outside for lateral entry in other levels. Disha also recommended the establishment and implementation of an enterprise-wide knowledge management portal.

Building Commitment

Regarding commitment building, the Disha design recommendations reinforced the continuation of the existing employee welfare systems that played a critical role in building employee commitment and maintaining the morale of the employees. Further, Disha HR Strategy design also made a few new recommendations. It proposed to focus on developing a reward and recognition system to build the ongoing commitment of employees to the organisation. Disha assessed the communication systems in NTPC and recommended to strengthen the communication matrix to enable better integration of the employees at the grassroots with the senior management.

Building Culture

On the framework of Culture Building, the HR strategy design took cognisance of the commendable work done in "Values Actualisation" through the creation of "Core Values Handbook" by NTPC HR. The proposed system envisaged values actualisation assessments to be done based on the details provided in the "Core Values Handbook". Disha also proposed a strong linkage of the "Values Actualisation" by individuals with the Performance Management System (PMS) and reward mechanisms. Needless to mention that adoption of the company's Core Values in business dealings has been an essential duty of executives at all levels. All executives are expected to have a significant role in the actualisation of Core Values by being 'Role Models' in observing and practicing them and thereby leading by example. Disha also developed a Culture Measurement Tool for periodic measurement of the organisational culture.

Building Systems

Regarding System Building, Disha recommended for continuation of the existing quality interventions such as Quality circles, suggestion scheme, benchmarking and 5S programs. Further, Disha found that there were several nagging issues in the Performance Management System such as lack of objectivity of the appraisal process for middle and junior management levels as it did not provide for pre-determination of KRAs and goals; non-congruity between the existing feedback systems and the existing policy relating to a comprehensive review and feedback process; non-provisioning of mechanism for periodic review, continuous feedback, mid-year review, communication of rating or providing performance feedback to the employees; and above all inefficiency of the process of moderation resulting in grade inflation, much above the normal distribution, at all levels.

Disha: NTPC Reinvents Itself

The recommendations of the Disha team were enumerated and presented to the management in December 2002. The implementation of the recommendations commenced in September 2004, after the Board of Directors accepted all the recommendations spanning all the areas on 16 July 2003 (Sinha, 2014).

Some of the salient points of implementation of Disha recommendations on Organisational Strategy are given herewith.

Commercial Function

As a first step towards strengthening its commercial processes and working closely with the customers, NTPC instituted the concept of Customer Relationship Management with the Regional Heads as "Customer Relationship Managers". Under the strengthened role, the Regional Heads discharged the role of being the primary window for interacting with the customer and corresponding regulatory agencies and became responsible for managing the "Customer Account".

Apart from managing commercial transactions for the sale of energy, the regions became responsible for marketing/supporting any other services that NTPC could offer. Dedicated "Customer Support Groups" were set up in the regions to identify and market such support services.

In addition, the commercial function at the region became responsible for tracking customer health and disseminating customer-related information within NTPC to facilitate planning and decision-making. This initiative helped in improving NTPC's customer interfacing skills and equipped NTPC to address the complexities of the customer environment. Another target benefit of the initiative was sensitisation of NTPC to the issues that customers are facing and help identify areas of collaboration with the customers.

The commercial function was vested with the added responsibility for safeguarding the rights of NTPC under the tripartite agreements as per the Montek Singh Ahluwalia recommendations and enforcing the security mechanisms due, in the event of default by any state utility.

NTPC strove to improve the speed of decision-making on commercial issues and ensure adequate representation of customer issues in the process. In this regard, NTPC instituted a central "Steering Committee" of all regional heads, along with their functional peers from finance, operations and corporate commercial. The steering committee became responsible for considering and recommending decisions to the management on matters of internal policy, customer support and collaboration, incentive schemes, etc. The inclusion of the regional heads in the steering committee ensured adequate representation for customer-facing issues and would drive greater responsiveness to the customer environment.

Fuel Management

The Fuel Management group, which was responsible for obtaining fuel linkages and signing agreements relating to fuel supply, also became responsible for the reduction of fuel costs and increasing the supply security for existing plants by seeking alternate sources of fuels and transportation mechanisms as well as for facilitating decisions on fuel choices for future plants. The group was also assigned with the responsibility for developing and executing business strategies and plans for diversification into coal mining and coal-washery. In doing this, they were assisted by New Business Development in Corporate Planning.

Global Footprint

To scout for more business opportunities in the Middle East, an office was opened in Dubai for Middle East business. Through this office, NTPC executed turnkey supply and installation/construction of 400 kV and 132 kV Transmission line and upgradation of existing 132 kV line to 400 kV for its client Dubai Electricity & Water Authority.

Integrated IT System

NTPC scrapped the legacy systems and implemented SAP to integrate the existing systems. It served the purpose of meeting the functionality requirements of all key business areas. It also provided scalability for a higher number of users and/or a number of stations. SAP provided multiple benefits to NTPC, such as higher employee productivity through IT-enabled processes, availability of real-time and accurate data for decision making, unified view of enterprise assisting in critical path analysis, aiding transparency across organisational processes and cost reduction.

Planning and Execution

The annual business planning process was rolled out which formed the basis for target setting and evaluation for plants, regions and functions. Further, project task forces were set up in Engineering Division and Project planning (pre- Zero date) was shifted to the Corporate Monitoring Group from Corporate Planning.

Realigned Regional Structure and Empowerment

Regional executive directors were empowered for quick decision-making facilitating smooth plant operations. Board sub-committees were restructured to increase the strategic focus of the Board, the scope of Management Committees (Executive Committees/Management Committees) was redefined; suitable changes were brought about in Delegation of Powers to support restructured business processes and decision-making, etc.

Diversification

NTPC made changes in its strategy and diversified the business portfolio along the energy value chain, as given herewith.

Hydro Power

Tapping into the vast hydropower resource in the country inspired NTPC to enter the hydro power business with the 800 MW Koldam hydro project in Himachal Pradesh. Two more projects were also taken up in Uttarakhand, viz. Tapovan-Vishnugad Hydro Power Project and Lata Tapovan Hydro Power Project.

Coal Mining

Pursuing a strategy of backward integration to create fuel security, NTPC ventured into the coal mining business.

Power Trading

'NTPC Vidyut Vyapar Nigam Ltd.' (NVVN), a wholly owned subsidiary, was created for trading power, leading to optimal utilisation of NTPC's assets.

Fly Ash Utilisation

Since ash was being used as a raw material by cement companies and brick manufacturers, NVVN was engaged in the business of fly ash export and sale to domestic customers.

Power Distribution

NTPC Electric Supply Company Ltd.' (NESCL), a wholly owned subsidiary of NTPC, was set up for distribution and supply of power.

Equipment Manufacturing

In order to augment power equipment manufacturing capacity, NTPC formed JVs with BHEL and Bharat Forge Ltd. for power plant equipment manufacturing. NTPC also acquired a stake in Transformers and Electricals Kerala Ltd. (TELK) for manufacturing and repair of transformers.

Renewable Power

To broad base its fuel mix NTPC planned for capacity addition of about 39 GW (i.e., around 30% of its capacity) through renewable resources, such as hydro, solar and wind energy by 2032.

In order to support the organisational changes recommended by Disha, NTPC also implemented the recommendations on diverse nuances of HR Strategy, as delineated herewith.

Building Competency

NTPC established and implemented an enterprise-wide knowledge management portal "Lakshya", based on Disha recommendations, to act as a mode of arranging, tracking and retrieving knowledge in NTPC. Lakshya offered a one-stop knowledge-sharing platform, making all available knowledge in the company, reachable at an integrated central source. A codified approach was followed while implementing the same. NTPC's engineers sent troubleshooting knowledge to Divisional Heads through emails and categories as per defined technical product lines and the same was made accessible through the web. This is how numerous technical troubleshooting tips and frequently asked questions (FAQs) were codified. A team of chief knowledge officer/domain leader/affinity groups was then formed through internal selections from among the existing employees to take care of the system.

Building Commitment

A bouquet of special Rewards and Recognition schemes was evolved with the objective of reinforcing good behaviour. The Rewards and Recognition Policy was brought about with the purpose of creating a culture of excellence with values actualisation, demonstration of leadership, fostering a culture of celebration and recognition, encourage overall development through involvement in total quality management and socio-cultural activities and the like.

Based on the recommendations, top-down and bottom-up communication processes were reviewed and strengthened in the organisation. Initiatives were taken to increase the interaction between the leadership team and the employees at the grassroots. Communication forums were provided for employees to voice their concerns and provide feedback to the organisation regarding motivation, morale and commitment.

Building Culture

Based on Disha recommendations, value actualisation was made an ingredient of the Performance Management process in NTPC and a percentage of weightage, while allocating KRAs and competencies, was mandatorily allocated to a demonstration of value-based behaviour. Value actualisation was assessed by observing the demonstrated behaviour of the executive in day-to-day business dealings. Initiatives were taken to enhance customer orientation and inculcate a culture of working based on the needs and expectations of the customers, internal as well as external. Customer inputs were incorporated in individual KRAs and customer orientation was made an index in individual dashboards. Further, based on the recommendations of Disha, several culture assessment tools/questionnaires such as Core Values actualisation, Employee Relations climate assessment Questionnaire, Rewards and Recognition Questionnaire, Services Effectiveness Questionnaire, etc. were designed and implemented. NTPC regularly conducts Employee Satisfaction and Organisational Climate Surveys.

Building Systems

Based on the recommendations of Disha, the Performance Management System was redesigned to change the focus from performance appraisal to performance management systems at all levels. Measures like key result areas, review and feedback system, communication of scores, identifying developmental needs and linking of rewards and recognition, etc. were undertaken. The normalisation process was re-vamped so that executives would be normalised at the plant, Regional Headquarters or Corporate Centre level depending on seniority grades, within a cluster, with a population of at least 15 executives, by the Performance Management Committees comprising cross-functional members, specifically set up for the purpose.

NTPC: Concluding Observations

Arnold (2000) suggests that "all history in some way wishes to say something about its own present time" and "the need to interpret the past, not simply present it". This extant case depicts how the basic tenets of the HR strategy in its four Building Blocks of Competency, Commitment, Culture and Systems Building had to undergo changes so the HR function supports the Organisational Transformation NTPC was undergoing during this period. The true value of historiographic research lies in ensuring that the readers build such analogies about things as are correct. Nibbling through history is a manifestation of an incessant search for patterns and an attempt to learn how such patterns can be duplicated from one situation to another through the changing times. This study presents substantial connections among phenomena to serve as an aid to understanding the role of HR in organisational transformation.

Some researchers have christened change programmes in public sector organisations as in the nature of 'relabelling' exercises, as organisations implement superficial changes, but spring back to their previous strategy and culture soon (Brunsson, 1989; Brunsson & Olsen, 1993). But as can be seen from the NTPC case, the organisational transformation exercise it underwent between 2002 and 2005 was so fundamental that it altered the very nature of NTPC's business and it transformed itself from a mere thermal power generating company to one doing business in the entire value chain of power. So much so the company had to change its nomenclature itself. In fact, the Disha recommendations were so central to the company that the name of National Thermal Power Corporation was changed to its present name NTPC Limited on 28 October 2005 to reflect the diversification of NTPC's business operations beyond thermal power generation to include, among others, generation of power from hydro, nuclear and renewable energy sources and undertaking coal mining and oil exploration activities (Company History, NTPC Ltd., 2019). Human Resource Strategy was to form the very bedrock on which the entire organisational transformation strategy was to rivet and NTPC's HR built befitting systems and processes to fulfil the requirements of the business.

3 Professionalisation of Family Business

Family businesses have caught the attention of researchers in recent times. Princeton University describes a family firm as a company that is wholly held and managed by the participants belonging to a single family (cited in Akbar, 2008). Wikipedia (Family Business, 2018) defines a family business as 'a commercial organization in which decision-making is influenced by multiple generations of a family – related by blood or marriage – who are closely identified with the firm through leadership or ownership'. Family business is defined as a company keenly owned and/or managed by more than one member of the same family (Akbar, 2008; Entrepreneur, 2021). A business firm is considered as a family firm in so far as its ownership and management are concentrated in one family unit and its members endeavour to maintain family-based affinity within the organisation (Akbar, 2008). Family businesses with ownership vested in family members as top executives are extensively prevalent both among small- and medium-scale enterprises and among large companies in not only developing countries, but developed countries as well (La Porta, Lopez-de-Silanes, & Shleifer, 1999). Many of the large companies run by families are existing in a few of the OECD countries, some of which are into their third, or later, generation, demonstrating huge spells of longevity (Zafft, n.d.).

The study of family firms and entrepreneurship is at a nascent stage and it derives heavily from other disciplines such as sociology, economics, psychology, corporate governance, finance and law. Sometimes socio-economic models have been resorted to describe different aspects of the family businesses (Barth, Gulbrandsen, & Schonea, 2005; Berghe & Carchon, 2003; Jensen & Meckling, 1976; Lester & Cannella, 2006; Mustakallio, Autio, & Zahra, 2002; Schulze, Lubatkin, & Dino, 2003; Suddaby & Jaskiewicz, 2020). Theories of psychology and sociology have been used to explore connections between family relations business goings-on and changing social and legal arrangements (James, 2006). Business historians have striven to appreciate the contribution of family

DOI: 10.4324/9781003191384-4

businesses to economic growth in both developing and developed countries (Colli, 2006). They have been investigating not only the divergent features of family firms vis-à-vis the dissimilar cultural mores, but the impact of the socio-economic milieu in shaping the structures, objectives, values and vision of such family firms (Colli & Perez, 2014).

Journey of Family Businesses and Role of HR

Some strands of literature on family businesses have emerged and grown over the last few decades (Astrachan, Zahra, & Sharma, 2003; Bird, Welsch, Astrachan, & Pistrui, 2002; Chrisman, Chua, & Litz, 2002; Daspit, Holt, Chrisman, & Long, 2016; Nordqvist, Sharma, & Chirico, 2014; Verbeke, Yuan, & Kano, 2019; Zahra & Sharma, 2004), which includes, succession, growth, corporate governance, stratagem, entrepreneurship, ethos, internationalisation and professionalisation. Among the many variegated reasons for such proliferation of interest apparently what stands out is a kind of response to the negativism of managerial capitalism. The plethora of corporate scandals at the turn of the twenty-first century brought into sharp focus the issues of stakeholder management, corporate governance and prototypes of proprietorship (Ahmed & Uddin, 2018; Chua, Chrisman, & Sharma, 1999; Mitchell, Agle, Chrisman, & Spence, 2011).

Longevity is a concept of paramount importance in the framework of family firms. The running of the business through family members posits opportunities, as well as threats and generates issues of possible imbalance. Such potent scenarios of disequilibrium greatly challenge one of the most important facets of family business, that is, the fact that such businesses are fundamentally possessions that are to be bequeathed from generation to generation. Longevity is thus a highly pertinent and strategic measure of performance in so far as family businesses are concerned (Colli, 2012).

Corporate governance – the process in which companies collect resources, the way power is delegated, and the way in which strategic decisions are taken – often determines the longevity or survival of family businesses as well as their propensity towards strategic positioning (Carney, 2005). Finer nuances of corporate governance on which research on family businesses is focusing on are delineated herewith:

> *Finance.* To meet the demands of growth, the family firms need to position themselves to raise capital. However, in the process, the risk of losing ownership, hitherto restricted to a limited number of kith and kin, runs rife. The legal issue the firm is faced with is to determine what kind of legal form the company should take (Gallo & Villaseca, 1996).

Ownership characteristics. Adaptability to the vagaries of market conditions is of paramount importance for the growth and survival of any company, more so in the dynamism of volatile technological developments (Chirico & Salvato, 2008). One view about family firms is their supposed tendency to conservatism and consequent inability to remain agile in times of need.

Cohesion. As family businesses grow, ownership and control tend to be shared among various members of the family. In such eventualities, one problem that may crop up is the divergence in strategic perceptions and conflicts of interests between the family lines, which could lead to sacrificing homogeneity (Ensley & Pearson, 2005). Joshi, Dixit, Sinha, and Shukla (2016) investigate the nature of conflicts that arise in a closely held family business and conclude that conflicts are paramount to forward progression for both the family and business when it is considered constructively.

In view of the multiple and diverse descriptions of family firms and the multifarious issues of corporate governance and longevity, Akbar (2008) adopts a method of categorising such firms based on the structural attributes of ownership and control of firms into a two-by-two matrix and characterises family businesses falling into four quadrants. According to Akbar (2008), the progression of professionalisation moves from quadrant I to quadrant IV through quadrants II and III. Similarly, the degree of concentration of ownership by family also moves in the same manner. In fact, the interplay of these twin factors determines the various facets of the family business, such as a system of corporate governance, strategy formulation and execution and performance outcome.

The companies falling in quadrant I are the unadulterated types of family businesses that own and regulate their businesses either by a sole proprietor or by members of a singular family or related families. Both financial and managerial control solely rests with the family. Most small companies belong to this category, which lacks transparency in their processes, at least to outsiders. They lack structures and systems and are governed by informal relations and communications.

As pure and unadulterated family businesses grow, outside investors move in, funding from banks and capital markets pour in and gradual formalisation sets in. Thus, the businesses falling in quadrant II are grown from the gyrations of the success attained by quadrant I companies. In such companies, the promoters-owners control the business through crossholding of equity, in addition to holding the board positions. The outside investors represent a minuscule minority of shareholders.

With greater maturity, more professionalisation sets in. Family businesses move from quadrant II to quadrant III. Even as the companies falling in quadrant III are owned by families, generally these are managed by professionals, more so at the operational level. In so far as the professionals so engaged are expected to act in the interests of the owners, the role of the latter boils down to ensuring reduction in agency problems, which in corporate finance refers to 'conflict of interest between a company's management and the company's stockholders' (Agency Problem, investopedia, 2019).

Gradually companies move to the stage of investor-driven firms, which are characterised by multi-divisional structures and direct investor holdings. Thus, the companies falling in quadrant IV have distributed investors, who have varying degrees of ownership of the firm. The Board of Directors handles the affairs of the company and manages the agency problems in the best interest of block equity holders. Most decisions, at both the transactional and strategic levels, are taken by professional managers.

Researchers have delved deep into related aspects of family businesses such as power asymmetry in agency theory, as by Saam (2007), agency cost and ownership structure, as by Ang, Cole, and Lin (2000), agency networks' conflict and cooperation, as by Mukherji, A, Wright, and Mukherji, J (2007), choice of management form contingent upon agency issues, as by Sirmans, G.S., Sirmans, C.F., and Turnbull (1999), stewardship theory in studying family business, as by Chrisman (2019), safeguarding the interests of minority shareholders in family businesses, as by de Holan and Sanz (2006), critical success factors for transitions of family firms, as by Morris, Williams, Allen, and Avila (1997), role of the business family learning in the longevity of family firms, as by Löhde, Calabrò, and Torchia (2020), state of voluntary corporate disclosure in family firms, as by Ali, Chen, and Radhakrishnan (2007), differences in productivity of family firms pursuant to changes in ownership regimes, as by Barth et al. (2005), agency relationship between employed professionals and the owners promoters, as by Rajan and Zingales (2001), transition of structures of corporate governance through the evolution of professionalisation process, as by Gedajlovic, Lubatkin, and Schulze (2004), etc.

Even as family businesses move through the progression of professionalisation from quadrant I to quadrant IV through quadrants II and III, they dialectically influence the various functions within the company, including HR. In fact, HR, being the function that inevitably is vested with inculcating the desired culture within the organisation, becomes one of the first functions to transform and bring about the organisational transformation on the journey of professionalism.

According to Vollmer and Mills (1965), a profession is an "ideal type or model of occupational structure characterised by certain specified elements," and professionalisation is the social process whereby an occupational group incorporates elements of this ideal type. The essential characteristics of this process of professionalisation of HR are the ethical orientation of HR and the body of specialised knowledge and skills which are required to perform the service of HR. Losey (1997, p. 147) asserts that 'human resource management is a profession' in so far as there is a body of knowledge that can be imparted, learned and tested and that there is an ethical code of conduct. It is perceived that the professionalisation of HR as a function involves setting up common standards of entry, performance and exits, known and standardised processes of codes of conduct and dealing with breaches thereof, benchmarked best practices regarding structures, systems and processes, definition and gaining of requisite levels of competencies, and the like. Walker (1988) avers that "HR people have to got to stop conceptualising their role as a 'professional' individual contributor and realise that their job is to help provide corporations with leadership on HR issues". In a report on a survey carried out by the Institute of Personnel Management in New Zealand in 1997, it is indicated that "it is irrelevant whether HR is a profession: what matters is whether HR practitioners behave in a professional manner" (Pajo & Cleland, 1997, p. 5). Increasing professionalisation thus necessarily implies augmentation of competencies in new arenas such as change management, influence and technology (Crouse, Doyle, & Young, 2011).

This case study explores the growth of Jindal Steel and Power Ltd. (JSPL) as a company on its journey of professionalism and how HR as a function has facilitated the journey by building up its own systems and processes.

JSPL: Saga of a Steel and Power Major in India

JSPL is an industrial powerhouse with a dominant presence in the steel, power, mining and infrastructure sectors. Part of the US$ 22 billion OP Jindal Group, this young, agile and responsive company is constantly expanding its capabilities to fuel its fairy tale journey that has seen it grow to a US$ 3.6 billion business conglomerate. The company has committed investments exceeding the US$ 30 billion in the future and has several business initiatives running simultaneously across continents.

The Jindal Group is constituted of four main companies. These companies are Jindal Stainless, Jindal Saw Ltd., Jindal Steel & Power Ltd. and JSW Steel Ltd. The steel behemoth is the sixth-largest business conglomerate in India in terms of assets. It was established in 1970 by Mr. O.P. Jindal, who was later joined in by his four sons: Mr. P.R. Jindal, Mr. Sajjan Jindal, Mr. Ratan Jindal and Mr. Naveen Jindal.

In 1998, Mr. O.P. Jindal assigned one of his four companies to each of his four sons. These second-generation leaders controlled and managed these companies independently, as if it were their own businesses and Mr. O.P. Jindal continued as the chairman of these companies. Jindal Saw was led by Mr. P.R. Jindal. Mr. Sajjan Jindal was vested with JSW Steel. Mr. Rattan Jindal was bestowed with the responsibility of Jindal Stainless, and Mr. Naveen Jindal with Jindal Steel & Power. However, all the brothers had equity shares in all four companies. Mr. O.P Jindal later demitted the position of chairperson of Jindal Saw and was succeeded by his eldest son P.R. Jindal but remained chairperson of the other three companies. The younger three sons were vice-chairpersons of the companies they steered.

Thus, Mr. O.P. Jindal had resolved a very intricate issue of succession of the family business during his lifetime itself. The intricacy of the issue of succession in family businesses can be gauged by the very fact that many articles on family business begin with the proclamation that fewer than 30% of family businesses are transferred on to the second generation and that only 10% make it to the third generation (Lansberg, 1999), and sometimes, it is averred that the average life span of a family business is 24 years, which is synchronous with the span that the founder exists at the rudder of the business (Welles, 1995). Further, several researchers have observed that there is no link between planning and successful succession (Aronoff, 1998; Astrachan, 2001; Keating & Little, 1997; Lansberg, 1999; Murray, 2003). They hold that succession is a one-time event, whereas transfer of a family business to the next generation is a lifelong and ongoing process. Bozer, Levin, and Santora (2017) have examined the issue of succession from a multidimensional perspective and identified many personal components, such as family-business socialisation and external experiences, that support the commitment of successors.

By assigning one each of his four companies to each of his four sons, Mr. O.P. Jindal, during his lifetime itself, had ensured a smooth transition of the family business to the next generation. Mr. O.P. Jindal unexpectedly expired in an aeroplane crash on 31 March 2005 and the Jindal Group suddenly became bereft of a head. Then, the four sons appointed their mother, Mrs. Savitri Jindal, as chairperson of all four companies in the group. The eldest son P.R. Jindal even stepped down from his position of chairperson in Jindal Saw for his mother and became vice-chairman. The four brothers' decision to appoint the mother as the chairwoman was a momentous strategic move.

Literature is surfeit with the role of the mother and many espouse that it can effectively watch over the shared family dream (Lansberg, 1999). Remaining in anonymity, the mother quite often plays a very significant role in the business (Muson, 2002). Mother has an important role in mediating the quality of the relationship between the founder and the successor (Bell & Pham, 2020). Poza and Messer (2001) distinguish six types of women in family businesses: jealous wife, chief emotional officer (CEO), business partner or co-entrepreneur, employee, guardian of the family values and a free agent. Whatever may be the role of a mother in a family business, Mrs. Savitri Jindal never took an active part in the business. The Group continued under the same structure as was prevalent during the lifetime of Mr. O.P. Jindal. Subsequently, in the third quarter of 2012, Naveen Jindal was formally christened as chairman of JSPL.

JSPL is one of India's fastest-growing and largest integrated steel manufacturers, with a significant presence in mining, power generation, oil and gas and infrastructure. As a long-term value creator, its endeavours are aligned with the government's make-in-India strategy. The equity shares of JSPL are listed on the Bombay Stock Exchange and the Jindal family holds 60% of equity.

Its vision is 'to be a globally admired organisation that enhances the quality of life of all stakeholders through sustainable industrial and business development' (Jindal Steel & Power, 2019). Jindalites aspire to achieve business excellence through a spirit of entrepreneurship and innovation, optimum utilisation of resources, sustainable environment-friendly procedures and practices, highest ethics and standards, hiring, developing and retaining the best people, maximising returns to stakeholders and positive impact on the communities.

The value sphere of Jindal comprises pillars encompassing all that is needed to constitute an ideal work environment. Its core values fall into the acronym 'POSSIBLE'; P – Passion for People, O – Ownership, S – Sustainable Development, S – Sense of Belonging, I – Integrity, B – Business Excellence, L – Loyalty.

When Mr. Naveen Jindal came back after completing his MBA from the University of Texas in 1992, he was put in charge of the group's ailing Raigarh plant in Chhattisgarh that required immediate interventions in terms of technologies to bring the organisation to a profiteering position. Mr. Naveen Jindal converted a tiny and ailing factory into Rs. 47,000 crore empire by investing in new technology and equipment.

He started with a focus on backward integration and worked for coal and iron ore acquisitions. After excelling in the field of steel, he entered Power, Oil and Gas sectors consecutively. Again, due to his focus on raw materials in 2008, he won four oil and gas exploration blocks in Georgia in a global bidding. He also headed other global ventures in Bolivia, South Asia and Africa.

Jindal's pipeline of new projects includes a hydro power joint venture with the state government of Arunachal Pradesh and an ambitious project to process liquid petroleum from high ash coal using German technology. Subsidiary Jindal Petroleum has secured seven oil blocks, five in Georgia and one each in Bolivia and India. A brief exposition of the various business verticals is given herewith.

The company has its business widespread, both nationally and internationally. In the national spheres, JSPL produces economical and efficient steel and power through backward and forward integration across the states of Chhattisgarh, Odisha and Jharkhand. The company not only continues to work concertedly to expand in its core areas, but is also diversifying into new businesses and has its presence in international areas of Africa, Australia, Oman (Middle East) and Indonesia. The company has a broad portfolio in steel, power, cement, mining and sponge iron.

The total income and profit after tax of JSPL since 2006–2007 are depicted in Appendix 4. Diminution of profit was because the Group was hit hard by rising interest burden and lower sales realisation and impacted by lower steel prices and the fuel crisis in the power business.

Steel prices have shown significant volatility in 2013, ranging from a high of $690 per tonne to a low of $586 per tonne. In the first half of 2014, steel prices rose steadily, continuing an upward trend beginning mid-2013. The second half of 2014 and complete 2015 demonstrated a significant decrease in steel prices, which stood at $353 per tonne by the end of 2015.

JSPL's coal-fired power project in Tamnar was the first-ever project in India to operate on a merchant power basis. This means that unlike other projects bound by tariffs fixed through long-term power purchase agreements (PPAs) with state governments, JPL was free to sell power at spot rates to any buyer in the market. The company's 1,000 MW plant turned fully operational in 2008.

Falling steel price realisations and demand and price volatility of power in the merchant market and lack of raw material integration coupled up to affect margins and this tough period coincided with obligations to repay debt. Delays in the company's plans to raise funds by selling assets, transferring certain assets to joint ventures and refinancing debt considerably got delayed increasing JSPL's woes. In the first week of May 2016, JSW Energy Limited had agreed to acquire a 1,000 MW(4X250) Thermal Power Plant, located at Tamnar, Raigarh, Chhatisgarh for Rs. 6,500 crore through an SPV arrangement. (JSW Energy to acquire JSPL's 1,000MW plant for Rs. 6,500 crore, Times of India, 4 May 2016.) However, since the plant continued operating at a plant load factor (PLF) up to 60 per cent by June 2019, and understandably, a plant operating at over 50 per cent PLF, can normally service its debt easily, JSW terminated its deal with Jindal Steel and Power (JSW Energy terminates Rs 6.5K deal to buy JSPL's 1 GW plant in Raigarh, the *Economic Times*, July 1, 2019).

Mr. Naveen Jindal has many facets to his personality. His dynamic persona reflects in his various roles as a representative of Kurukshetra in the 14th and 15th Lok Sabha, the chairman of Jindal Steel and Power Limited

(JSPL), Chancellor of the O.P. Jindal Global University, President of the Flag Foundation of India, a sports enthusiast and a family man. He is a steel visionary and a former Member of Parliament and Minister for Power in the State of Haryana. He is the man behind the transformation of a moderately performing company into a world-class organisation. He has also been ranked as India's Best CEO by *Business Today* based on a BT-INSEAD-HBR study of top value creators for the period 1995 to 2011.

Mr. Naveen is not only a successful entrepreneur but also a caring politician, a compassionate social servant and an effective parliamentarian. He is open to innovative approaches through either written sources or his own employees. He believes in a public expression of emotions as a driving force to bring about change. Regarding his long battle to hoist the National Flag as a fundamental right, he says, "Have you ever held the Indian flag? The feeling of hoisting the flag is difficult to express in words" (Education is a philanthropic effort and not business for us, Financial Express, 17 June 2012).

Mr. Naveen Jindal is well known to be a participative leader among his colleagues, employees and in society. He himself says, "In business I address my weakness by putting in charge people who possess the relevant strengths. Individual sports do not allow you to do that. You need to have a good mix of people so that different ideas get thrown in all the time and allows for a balanced approach" (JSPL MD Naveen Jindal, The Economic Times, 24 August 2012).

Project Drishti

A major organisational re-structuring exercise (Project Drishti) was carried out with the help of Accenture in 2007. The broad imperatives which led to the re-structuring exercise were growth, sustainability, transitioning from family-run business to a professionally run organisation and operational excellence. The averred objectives of the initiative were spelled out: to have significant cost reduction focus; to have a constant focus on cost as the cyclical nature of the industry warrants the same; to have more process orientation as was necessitated within the overall structure; and to have a progressive movement to a shared services model.

A company's operating model is defined by the roles assigned to three basic organisational spheres and the processes by which they interact to drive value:

> *A Corporate Core*. This consists of primary strategy, policy and oversight functions, delegated extension of CEO and Board of Directors and management of performance accountabilities for lines of business and support services delivery organisations.

Support Services*. This includes expertise/specialist services and back-office transactional support, that support lines of business and the corporate core based on cost/service trade-offs and documented through Service Level Agreements.

The Business Units*. These units are primary revenue-generating activities aligned to competitive and market requirements and utilise support services and operate under the direction of the Corporate Core.

Based on this, a Balanced Shared services operating model was designed for the domestic business, as depicted in Figure 3.1.

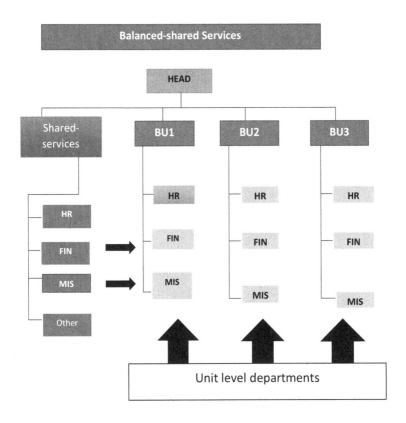

N.B: BU - Business Unit, MFG - Manufacturing, MKTG - Marketing, FIN – Finance, MIS - Miscellaneous

Figure 3.1 JSPL: Balanced Shared Services Operating Model

The rationale for a Balanced Shared services operating model for the domestic business was leveraging economies of scale, standardisation of services, focused skill-building, elimination of redundancies, enabling business units to focus on the core activity of operations, enabling future expansions benefitting from the centralised replicable model, providing growth avenues for the people in support functions and creating centres of service expertise.

Further, a fully decentralised operating model was adopted for overseas businesses. It was based on the premise that various geographic locations would have divergent complex issues, and it would be expedient to leverage the local resources and manage expectations of the local government and meet statutory requirements. Further, there would be difficulty in coordination of units at far-flung locations, and a fully decentralised operating model would help resolve such issues of co-ordination. The structure design is depicted in Figure 3.2:

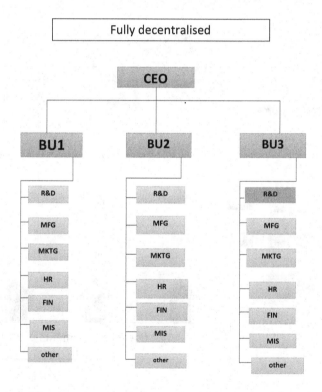

N.B: BU - Business Unit, MFG - Manufacturing, MKTG - Marketing, FIN – Finance, MIS – Management Information System

Figure 3.2 JSPL: Fully Decentralised Overseas Structure

Thus, the top-line organisational structure that emerged is given in Figure 3.3:

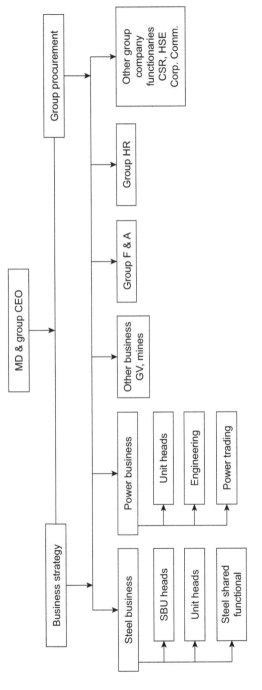

Figure 3.3 JSPL's Topline Organisational Structure

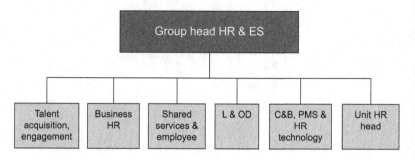

Figure 3.4 JSPL: HR Structure

Restructuring of HR

The restructured HR structure is portrayed in Figure 3.4.

Following positions directly report to the head of corporate HR:

- Recruitment Head – responsible for setting recruitment policy and top management recruitment
- Training & Development & Performance Management System (PMS) Head – responsible for setting Training and Development (T&D) and PMS policy and monitoring performance on Training and PMS implementation.
- Unit Personnel & Organisational Development Head, Raigarh – Responsible for all HR activities at JSPL, Raigarh, Jindal Power Ltd. (JPL), Tamnar, Mines and Machinery Division Raipur. This position also has a dotted line reporting to the Unit head Raigarh
- Site Personnel & Organisational Development Head, Angul and Patratu – Responsible for all HR activities at the project site. Also has a dotted line reporting to the site project head.
- Security Head – Responsible for providing security services at all plants, recruiting and training security personnel. The position will be based out of Raigarh.

Project Nav Tarang

JSPL's incessant search for transformation into a benchmark institution led the Group to another organisational renewal exercise in 2010 named Project Nav Tarang, which was carried out with the assistance of Mckinsey, the global management consulting firm.

Based on the recommendations of the Mckinsey and in an endeavour to transform JSPL into a benchmark institution, it introduced a strategic planning process for defining long-term group and business strategies every 3 years, review business strategies and prioritise initiatives annually, and defining key metrics and milestones for performance measurement on a quarterly basis. The key outputs of the process were long-term (5–10 years) group and business strategy with standardised business cases for all strategic initiatives every 3 years, annual operating plan for each business, including defining resource requirements, and quarterly de-bottlenecking of issues related to strategic initiatives. The main themes of the long-term strategy, as it emerged, were, accelerate base load capacity addition while locking in domestic coal, capture profit pools from peaking power, create options in renewables and build organisation and strengthen key capabilities.

An appropriate review process was also implemented. The Group Council (GC) review was assigned to take up review of business performance and problem-solving and de-bottlenecking on business head-level issues. The Management Committee review was to deal with operating plants' performance, review projects for progress on time and cost, debottlenecking key issues, disseminating best practices and preparing for Group Council review. Operation Review and Project Review Teams (ORT/PRT) were entrusted with a detailed package-by-package review, status check of key execution milestones, and address key bottlenecks and develop a mitigation plan.

The internal audit process was revamped. The internal audit team was completely insulated from businesses and was allocated an independent career path. It was empowered with direct reporting to the Joint Managing Director and was assigned to have monthly reviews at the level of Group Council. All relevant departments were assigned to define clear guidelines/ Standard operating Processes for audit. Adequate risk-based controls were also established across the group.

Delegation of powers was introduced with the objective of empowerment of business/ function heads, facilitation of timely and constructive inputs for better decisions and faster decision-making, and for exercising adequate controls/checks. The design principles behind the delegation of powers were to have a robust budgeting process as the foundation for effective and fast financial approvals, differentiation based on budgeted versus non-budgeted (ad-hoc) spend, within budget versus over-budget limits, nature of award of contract depending upon the number of parties involved.

HR's Synchronisation in the Transformational Voyage

To prop up the organisational transitioning process evolved in 2007 and 2010, appropriate HR systems and processes were also sought to be designed in the Project Drishti and Project Nav Tarang. Salient points of a few of such HR interventions are given herewith.

Jindal Lead Management Group (JLMG)

To attract and recruit high-potential employees for JSPL, groom talent for a career of life-long mobility across industries and functions, develop a leadership pipeline for the organisation and provide an accelerated career path to high-potential existing employees, the scheme of Jindal Lead Management Group was implemented in 2007. Shortlisting of internal candidates is done based on openings in JLMG and subject to the eligibility of a minimum 2 years' service in JSPL, performance rating of at least "Exceeded Expectations" and age being less than 28. Short listing Process for external candidates is done through JLMG Aptitude Test (JAT) on the lines of Common Admission Test (CAT), testing analytical skills, reading comprehension, verbal ability, quantitative ability, data interpretation and sufficiency, logical reasoning and general knowledge/current affairs.

All JLMG employees join at Raigarh for the 1-month induction course. Each trainee is allocated a mentor during the induction. The mentor supports the trainee till the end of the training. The mentor's role is primarily to provide guidance, solve issues and motivate the trainee. JLMG Cadre employees are confirmed after one year of training as managers. They are put on a fast-track career path with the objective of grooming them quickly to assume leadership positions. The career path of JLMG candidates takes them to Career Level 2 in about 10 years of joining. Thus, around the age of 35, the JLMG cadre employees become Associate Vice President (AVP). At each promotion point, JLMG cadre employees are evaluated based on their performance and demonstration of leadership competencies. At promotion points where the career level changes, evaluation of leadership competencies is for proficiency levels required at the next career level. The assessment is carried out by an expert panel organised by the JLMG coordinator. Total nine batches of Jindal Lead Management Group employees have been recruited under the scheme.

Performance Development and Review Process

Performance Development and Review (PDR) process was launched with the avowed objective to set performance standards and goals, communicate performance expectations, support employees in accomplishing set goals and evaluate the impact/outcome of the employee's performance. It consists of four stages, that is, goal setting, mid-year performance review, annual appraisal and action on performance results. During the goal-setting phase, the reporting officer explains to the employee what the PDR process is, defines roles, discusses job requirements, answers the employee's questions about the PDR process, and works with the employee to reach a consensus on and commitment to performance standards. By the end of the discussion, 5–10 key result areas are identified, measurement criteria for each are ascertained and targets and weightage are allocated to each of the goals. The mid-year review at JSPL takes place in the form of a discussion between the reporting officer and employee to ascertain the progress on goals and behavioural skills. An annual appraisal at JSPL is the culminating discussion between the reporting officer and staff member regarding where performance exceeded, met, or fell below expectations, the learning and development needed and received, goals that were set and achieved by the employee, and feedback from others affected by the employee's performance.

Behavioural Competency Framework

A Behavioural Competency Framework has been designed in JSPL to articulate the expectations on behaviours and attitudes from employees, highlight "soft" skills required when defining job expectations and reflect on corporate values and strategic priorities. The competencies identified are Action and Result orientation, Initiative, Communication, Adaptability and Flexibility, Managing Change, Building Best People, Customer Orientation, Interpersonal Relations, Teamwork, Business Knowledge, Business Performance Measurement, Cost and Profitability Orientation, Data Gathering and Analysis, Decision-Making, Problem-Solving, Strategic Thinking, Planning and Organizing and Quality Orientation which are measured on five proficiency levels such as Basic, Application, Proficient, Advance and Expert. Depending on the career levels clubbed into different clusters, viz. visionary, strategic, tactical, and operational or executioner, the desired proficient levels of the competencies are measured.

Career Development Scheme

JSPL rolled out a Career Development Scheme for Career Growth of Employees in the Executive cadre in the year 2010. The organisational hierarchy was grouped into five different bands based on the people management responsibilities in each band, viz. enterprise managers, business managers, functional managers, manage others and manage self. Specific growth framework depending on Performance and Potential Rating, Qualification, Evaluation through appropriate Committees, etc. was delineated for within band and interband promotions.

Succession Planning

A Succession Planning process was also rolled out for the employees in the executive cadre in all the Group Companies. As per the scheme, at least one immediate successor (capable of succeeding incumbent in 0–1 year) and one down-the-line successor (capable of succeeding incumbent in 1–3 years) need to be identified and nurtured for all the critical positions in the organisation.

JSPL: Concluding Observations

Professionalisation of a family business is a journey from pure family firms to organisations managed through and by professionals. Family businesses as they traverse through time find themselves at different levels of professionalisation. HR, being the function that inevitably is vested with inculcating the desired culture within the organisation, becomes one of the initial functions to transform and bring about the organisational transformation on the journey of professionalism. It is perceived that the professionalisation of HR as a function involves setting up common standards of entry, performance and exits, known and standardised processes of codes of conduct and dealing with breaches thereof, benchmarked best practices regarding structures, systems and processes, definition and gaining of requisite levels of competencies, and the like. JSPL HR has played its role in bringing about the desired changes and professionalism in the company to meet the requirements of a business.

4 Changing Contours of Unionism and HR as an Enabler

Participative Management is one of the High Performing Work Practices (HPWPs) being pursued in many organisations in modern days. Even as Participative Management is a generic term involving participation of all sections of employees, viz. executives and non-executives, in India, in the context of Employee Relations, it is specifically used as Workers' Participation in Management. Trade Unions are perceived as an important instrumentality for creating efficacious situations leading to effective participatory management. Diverse situational factors of current-day business scenario have converged to bring in transition of the roles of trade unions from primarily bargaining institutions to specialised organisations, focused on representing the interests of labour for betterment of Quality of Work Life (QWL).

This case study captures the process of participative management and the changing role of Trade Unions from collective bargaining to improving the quality of lives of workers and non-executives in the context of the National Aluminium Company (NALCO).

Workers' Participation in Management and Changing Role of Trade Unions

The term Workers' Participation in Management (WPM) is interpreted differently by involved parties. For management, it comprises of joint consultation prior to decision-making, for workers, it implies co-determination, while for government, it is the involvement of labour with management, without the final authority or responsibility in decision-making.

Historically, it has been observed that unions in general have sought to indorse collective bargaining rather than workers' participation in management. In India, workers' participation is structurally in-built in statute. Under the provisions of the Industrial Disputes Act, Works Committees are to be formed to investigate the points of discord between the

DOI: 10.4324/9781003191384-5

employer and the employees in the day-to-day working of the institution and to promote methods of fortifying amity and harmonious relations between them.

Collective bargaining is a mode of joint regulation by employers and workers' organisations. Respect for rules emanates from the manner of their formulation. Collective bargaining is a process of rule formulation through mutual consent. Often collective bargaining is viewed as a process of unions' sharing of governance with management. It is a process in which the terms and conditions of employment are determined jointly by the employer and workers.

The main objective of collective bargaining is the co-determination of terms and conditions of employment through discussions and negotiations and the process of give-and-take. As the terms of employment and the conditions of work-life have broadened through the evolution of time, so also has the gamut of collective bargaining.

Collective bargaining is limited not only to employer and workers, but the state also plays a notable mandatory role in regulating various characteristics of collective bargaining (Remesh, 2017). Some of these are selecting bargaining agent, shaping the enforceability of collective bi-partite or tripartite settlements, putting obligations on the employer and trade unions to bargain collectively and placing restrictions on industrial actions in the eventuality of failure of negotiations. With changing times, the basic characteristics of collective bargaining are also changing.

If participatory decision-making is a resultant of how employees use the instrumentalities for collective participation efficacy to create situations conducive to their effectiveness (Mitchell, 1973), Trade Unions are perceived as an important instrumentality for creating such efficacy. A trade union, thus, is an organisation designed by non-executives and workers primarily to guard their interests and ameliorate their working conditions. It is a continuous association of wage earners for maintaining and improving working conditions (Dankert, 1948). According to Ghosh and Geetika (2007), protection of basic worker and human rights in developing nations dictates unionisation in order that the workers gainfully share the benefits of economic growth.

The primary function of a trade union is to uphold and protect the interest of its members (Hoxie, 1921; Perlman, 1928). This can be summarised as follows:

i.   To improve working and living conditions and to represent workers' interests in various fora (Freeman & Medoff, 1984).
ii. To offer cooperation in improving levels of safety, production and productivity, discipline and quality.

iii. To secure fair wages for workers. Madheswaran and Shanmugam (2003) studied the influence of trade unions on wages by guesstimating the union–non-union wage disparity using a single wage equation, considering unionism as a dummy. They estimate that workers within the unionised sector earn 19% more than the workers in the non-unionised sector.

iv. To promote identity of workers' interests with their industries.

vi. To enlarge opportunities for promotion and training.

After independence, initially for around 30 years, there was heightened stress on centralised bargaining, because of the enormous role of the State in labour market institutions. Industrial relations fulfilled the role of providing employees with a common forum to put forth their views and demands, and unions with the wherewithal to establish standardised terms and conditions of employment within both an enterprise and an industry (Nimbalkar, 2019). This had positive effect on wages (D'Souza, 1998), even though it has sometimes been felt that during this period centralised bargaining had become a tool for political chicanery, as wages and working conditions were often decided entirely on political considerations (Fonseca, 1964; Jackson, 1972; Myers, 1958).

A study by Ratnam (1999) shows that the phenomenon of collective bargaining has been on the wane because of:

a. The reduction in the size of the organised sector;
b. Capital intensity of industry;
c. Government giving permission for closing of businesses and decreasing employment through retrenchment and voluntary retirement schemes (VRS);
d. Promotion of export processing Special Economic Zones where labour rights exist only on paper;
e. Critical need of the management to effect fast economic growth in the wake of liberalisation and globalisation and consequent competition;
f. Government's passivism in matters of labour law violations.

Mahadevan (2000) has observed that with the ushering in of new economic policies leading to intense national and international competition, the employers have become constrained to minimise redundancies, shift to capital intensive mode and strive to have a lean organisation. They increasingly resort to shifting of jobs from the domain of bargaining to sub-contracting, deployment of contract labour, changing norms of work life, reducing jobs and moving towards a capital-intensive growth model. Excessive deployment of employees in project mode, employment of temporary workers on unceasing basis, outsourcing of non-core operations to service providers and assignation of workers through placement agencies are common practices being followed, even by public sector organisations. In short, there has been a growing process of "informalization of work within the formal sector" (Remesh, 2017).

Managements have continually felt that the statutes governing industrial relations have increasingly become archaic and obsolete and restrict organisations' ability to compete in the nationally and internationally competitive scenario. No attempt has been made by successive governments to reorient the laws relating to industrial relations and labour laws (Sodhi, 1994).

Even as in India collective bargaining has always remained limited in scope and restricted to the formal sector only (Rani & Sen, 2018), its contours have also sometimes changed at the behest of the management. Various ramifications of such changes have been the preference of management for enterprise-level bargaining, tendering of managements' charter of demands upon receiving the same from the unions and managements' persistence on discussing and resolving them either before or simultaneous to taking up union's demands, inclusion of measures of cost cutting, manpower rationalisation, productivity increases, pay for performance and technological upgradation in such managerial charters of demands (Sodhi, 1994).

Many industrial relations researchers have observed that the wideranging implementation of human resource management (HRM) practices across many contemporary workplaces is correlated with the concomitant weakening of unions (Kim, 2017). Often managements reorient their human resource policies making them look after the interests of the workers which hitherto has had been in the domain of the unions (Sodhi, 1999). Further, innovative HRM practices put a danger to trade unions in four ways: segmentation of work force and individualisation of employment contract, decrease of union representation, increase of work and decline of union solidarity by enhancing organisational commitment (Bratton, 1999).

Ahn (2010) has emphasised some of the factors contributing to the phenomenon of decline in collective bargaining which are:

a. Lack of legal proviso for recognition of trade unions as sole bargaining agent;
b. Multiplicity and lack of consensus among registered trade unions;
c. Increasing sophistication and deployment of state-of-the-art HR tools by Human Resource Managers, which has rendered redundant some of the functions of the trade unions;
d. Employment of flexi labour like contract, casual, part-time, need-based and contingent workers.

All this has resulted in the decline of trade unions' role and importance (Ratnam, 2007; Sankaran, 2007).

Rapid technological changes and successive revisions in pay have certainly upgraded workers' conditions within the organised sector, but generally at the cost of loss of control over jobs (Pattnaik, 2020; Ratnam, 2006). Other factors such as structural changes (Ellguth & Kohaut, 2019), technological changes (Meyer & Biegert, 2019) and economic growth and a continuous escalation in capital intensity, in both the product and labour markets (Jose, 1999) have brought in a paradigm shift in the roles of trade unions from primarily bargaining institutions to specialised organisations, focused on representing the interests of labour for betterment of QWL. Now, unionisation has assumed the role of bringing in improvement in the QWL of workers and non-executives (Ghosh & Geetika, 2007).

Thus, QWL is influenced by union–management relations (Sayeed & Sinha, 1981). The union's combined voice provides management with information on workplace and shop-floor issues, thus becoming a conduit of communication. This in turn facilitates sound and efficacious decision-making with respect to the day-to-day work life of the employees.

About the Modern Industrial "Konark"

National Aluminium Company Limited (NALCO), otherwise known among the people of Odisha as modern industrial "Konark", is a central public sector undertaking and has been conferred with Navratna status. It was incorporated in 1981 under the Department of Mines, Ministry of Steel and Mines, the Government of India. The company is a group "A" Central Public Sector Enterprise, with diversified operations encompassing bauxite mining, alumina refining, aluminium smelting and casting, power generation and rail and port operations. Presently, 51.5% equity of NALCO is vested with the Government of India (NALCO, 2020).

NALCO has its corporate office at Bhubaneswar, the state capital of Odisha. The company operates through the following segments: 68.25 lakh TPA Bauxite Mine (Panchpatmali in Koraput district), 21.00 lakh TPA Alumina Refinery (Damanjodi), 4.60 lakh TPA aluminium Smelter Plant (Anugul in Dhenkanal district), 1,200 MW Captive Power Plant (Anugul) and Port facilities (Visakhapatnam). Different segments of these businesses have gone into production/generation in a phased manner beginning from 1985.

Aligning with the ambitious programmes of the Government of India, the company is engaged in harnessing renewable energy. It has commissioned wind power plants of 50.4 MW at Gandikota, Andhra Pradesh, and of 47.6 MW at Jaisalmer, Rajasthan. 260 KWp Rooftop Solar Power System has been operationalised at the Corporate Office and Township, Bhubaneswar.

In total, the company has already commissioned 198 MW wind power plants and further 25 MW wind power plants are in pipeline.

NALCO has regional marketing offices in Delhi, Kolkata, Mumbai and Chennai, and branch offices at Bangalore, Paradeep and Ahmedabad and has 11 stockyards at various locations in India. All the manufacturing and port facilities are certified under ISO 9001, ISO 14001, and OHSAS 18001 Management Systems. Smelter, CPP and Alumina Refinery are also certified under ISO 50001 Standard for the energy management system.

The vision statement of NALCO is "To be a Premier and Integrated company in the Aluminium value chain with strategic presence in Mining both domestic & global, Metals and Energy sectors". Its mission is "To sustainably grow multi-fold in Mining, Alumina and Aluminium business along with select diversification in Minerals, Metals and Energy sectors, while continuously improving on efficiency and business practices thus enhancing value for all stakeholders". Its core values are encapsulated in the acronym BEST: viz. Benefitting Stakeholders, Excellence and quality, Sustainability and Trust & Integrity.

Total income and profit after tax of NALCO from 2006 to 2007 is presented in Appendix 4.

Employee Relations and HR at NALCO: Systems, Policies and Processes

The 38th Annual Report of NALCO reads,

> The Industrial Relations scenario of your Company reached the pinnacle of glory during the year 2018–19 by successfully providing a climate conducive to record performances on all fronts. The process of recognition of majority trade unions in different Units/Corporate Office was completed peacefully. After this, your Company finalised the Sixth Long Term Wage Settlement for non-executive employees for 10 years period from 01/01/2017 in a record time of about three months and only nine sittings in a very peaceful. and cordial atmosphere. The settlement complies with the applicable Government guidelines and has been finalised in the course of conciliation proceeding under the Industrial Disputes Act, 1947. There was no loss of man-days due to any Industrial Relations problem during the year.

Several registered unions function in all the units of NALCO. For recognition of Trade Union in NALCO, the Orissa State, implementation & Evaluation Committee (as provided in Verification of Membership and Recognition of Trade Union Rules, 1994) headed by Labour Commissioner of

Odisha as Member Secretary, passes a resolution recommending recognition through voting by secret ballot. This resolution is notified in the gazette of the Government of Odisha as required. Various Unions and their areas of operation along with affiliations to Central Trade Unions, if any, and Unit-wise status of recognition is given in Appendix 5.

The management has defined the facilities to be extended to unions in a structured form to bring in transparency. The facilities being extended to Recognised Trade Union vis-à-vis Unrecognised Trade Unions are given in Table 4.1.

Effective communication is essential to the implementation of organisational initiatives and for bringing in the desired change effects (DiFonzo &

Table 4.1 Facilities Extended to Unions in NALCO

Items	Recognised Unions	Unrecognised Unions	Remarks
Financial Assistance - Purpose: Annual Function, Labour Day Celebration, Public Awareness Programme, etc.	Rs. 2,00,000 plus the amount calculated at a rate Rs. 50 per member of votes polled in the last verification process	Rs. 65,000 plus the amount calculated at a rate Rs. 50 per member of votes polled in the last verification process	Unions securing 30% or more votes at the secret ballot
		Rs. 20,000 plus the amount calculated at a rate Rs. 50 per member of votes polled in the last verification process	Unions securing 10% or more votes but less than 30% of votes at the secret ballot
		Nil	Unions securing less than 10% votes
Training Programme (Leadership Development Programme – minimum of 2 days duration)	Maximum 100 man-days per year	• 50 man days per year (securing more than 30% votes) • 15 man days per year (securing more than 10% votes)	

(Continued)

Table 4.1 (Continued)

Items	Recognised Unions	Unrecognised Unions	Remarks
Office Space Size of	Up to 1,000 square feet	Office space to be decided by the unit depending upon the availability of space	Rs. 200 as license fee per annum to be charged towards rent, water, etc.
Official Tour	Maximum of 30 man days per year excluding journey	No tour	• No tour for visit to any place of the company or to State/Central or Dist. Head Quarters to discuss about the affairs of the Unions, to follow up certain issues relating to employees and to attend any function of the Central affiliated body at State or Central Level.
			Does not count for attending any structured meeting with the Management through official invitation or any training programme organised by the management.
Special Casual Leave	A total of 30 man-days in a year	15 man-days in a year	For attending annual functions/conventions/ seminar/conference/ symposium/workshop at the State/Central level by the Central Trade Union Organisations/Central Body.
Intercom Telephone + P&T Telephone to Office + Cell Phone to Secretary and President + Rs. 600 per month as phone reimbursement.	Minimum 08 intercoms + some additional IC telephone following fixed formulae (1 for every 20 members)	01 no. intercom to the Office of the Union(s) where the office space has been provided. (1 for every 20 members)	

Bordia, 1998; Lewis & Seibold, 1998; Schweiger & Denisi, 1991; Stacho, Stachová, Papula, Papulová, & Kohnová, 2019). Communication is vital to understanding issues organisations face to meet the challenges, and need to change (Bennebroek Gravenhorst, Werkman, & Boonstra, 1999; Odor, 2018). Shrivastava (2012) has also highlighted the role of communication in an organisation as well as in multidimensional business interactions.

Looking at the importance of communication in organisational efficacy and change management, NALCO has prepared a structure of Interaction with Recognised Unions/Associations, which is presented in Table 4.2.

Table 4.2 Structure of Interaction With Recognised Unions

Unions/ assn.	Unit level	Complex level	Corporate level	Apex level
	(Meeting in every Month)	*(Meeting in every alternate Month)*	*(Quarterly Meeting)*	*(Twice Meeting in a Year)*
Recognised union	Every month (6 union rep) unit head, HRD Chief, HOD of Finance, head of (O&M), HR Executive as secretary	Every second month in place of monthly unit level meeting Head of complex, unit heads, HRD chief, finance chief, HRD chiefs of units, HRD Executives dealing IR of both units. HRD Chief of the complex conduct meeting in every alternate month (5 reps. of each recognised unions of units)	Once in every 4 months (4 union rep) dir.(p&a), dir(p), HRD chief of corporate, HRD chief of complex, finance chief, HRD chiefs of units, HRD Executives dealing IR	Once in every 6 months of the financial year (2 union representatives of recognised unions of the company, all FDs, chief of the complex, HRD Chief of the complex and the corporate.
Officers' Association		Quarterly (6 rep) Head of complex, unit heads, HRD Chief, finance chief, HRD chiefs of units, rep. from other Depts, as per requirement	Once in 4 months (4 rep. of each assn.) dir. (p&a), dir(p), HRD chief of corporate, HRD chief of complex, finance chief, HRD chiefs of units	

(Continued)

Table 4.2 (Continued)

Unions/ assn.	Unit level	Complex level	Corporate level	Apex level
	(Meeting in every Month)	*(Meeting in every alternate Month)*	*(Quarterly Meeting)*	*(Twice Meeting in a Year)*
SC/ST employees Welfare Association		Once in 4 months (6 rep. of assn.) chief of complex, HRD chiefs of units, liaison officers of the units	Once in 6 months (4 rep. of each assn.) dir(p&a), chief of complex, HRD chiefs of units, chief liaison officer, liaison officers of the units	

Employees are the main force behind driving the organisation on the road of success. It is important for every organisation not only to look after the welfare of employees, but to listen to their voices as well so that they can also contribute to decision-making at various levels for betterment of the organisation. In order to bring about a sense of involvement and effective participation amongst the employees at various levels, towards a coordinated and determined effort for better all-round performance and improved efficiency, it is imperative to provide institutionalised forums for joint participation/consultation of the employees. This would help in the timely completion of interventions and the smooth functioning of the organisation.

Employee participation in management has been designed in NALCO to improve the participation level of employees to promote a better understanding between the management and its employees, inculcate a spirit of cooperation for maximising production and productivity and to motivate the workers and give them a greater sense of identity, belongingness and involvement in the organisational activities. Its broad objectives are to create a sense of oneness with the organisation and drive home the feeling of involvement; to sensitise employees about the various measures being taken for improving their working and living conditions and to make use of the valuable suggestions put forth by the employees for the benefit of the organisation and the personnel working in it.

The structure of Workers' Participation in Management is three-tier: Shop floor level, Unit level and Apex level. These committees consist of both Management and Workers' representatives. In these, discussions take place at bi-partite level. The workers' representatives are nominated by the respective Recognised Union of the unit. The various fora currently existing for participative management and a brief exposition of their functioning are given herewith.

Safety Committee

The objective of the Safety Committee is to create safety consciousness among employees and suggest ways and measures to the management for creating safe working conditions and bringing in a safe working culture. It is composed of eight representatives each from workers and management, along with chairman and convener. Its tenure is one year. The committee closely observes and advises on safety, accident prevention and housekeeping. The frequency of meetings is once a month.

Canteen Committee

It consists of four representatives from management and eight representatives from workers. Its tenure is 2 years. The committee closely monitors canteen facilities, cleanliness, cost and quality of raw materials, food being served and menu to be served and renders necessary actions for improvement. The committee meets once a month.

Welfare Committee

It consists of four members from management and eight members from workmen. This committee has a fixed tenure of one year after which it is reconstituted. The committee closely observes different welfare facilities extended by the management and suggests measures for improvement. The frequency of its meetings is once a month.

Grievance Committee

It consists of four members each from management and workmen. Its tenure is one year. The committee looks after the grievances of employees and ensures their prompt redressal. It meets as and when required, depending on the number of grievances received.

Shop Councils

The number of members of management and workmen of different Shop Councils varies from department to department. The Shop Councils closely observe production, productivity, improvement in working conditions and methods of working, prevention of wastage, cost control, pollution control, encouraging employees for useful suggestions, etc. The frequency of meetings of Shop Councils is once a month.

NALCO: Concluding Observations

From the entire gamut of issues, it transpires that trade unions at NALCO are as much involved in improving the QWL of employees, as in maintaining good industrial relations. Roles that were earlier considered secondary ones with respect to Unions have eclipsed the earlier roles of collective bargaining. The unions have been metamorphosed as watchdogs of welfare measures and QWL. Partnering in the day-to-day activities in the organisation not only through Participatory Fora, but ensuring an assiduous implementation of the communication matrix, thrusts the Unions into their new role of "Partners in Progress". HR can and does facilitate this transition by building appropriate policies, processes and systems and by strictly adhering to the same, as in the case of NALCO.

5 HR's Strategic Interventions

A Study Against Miles and Snow's Typology

This case study examines the organisational strategy of L&T Electrical & Automation (E&A) against the backdrop of Miles and Snow (1978) model and explores how the functional HR strategy integrates with the organisational strategy.

P-A-D-R Strategy Model and HR

Miles and Snow (1978) envisaged strategy as a conglomerate of decisions through which a strategic business unit integrates its managerial processes and capabilities with its business environment. Against this paradigm, businesses were conceptually categorised on the basis of their decision patterns into Prospector–Analyser–Defender–Reactor (P-A-D-R) model.

Prospectors are technologically innovative. An organisation that follows a prospector strategy is characterised as one which is highly innovative and is constantly looking for new markets and new business opportunities. It is consistently concerned with growth and pursues a culture of risk taking.

Analysers tend to prefer a "second-but-better" strategy. An organisation that pursues an analyser strategy not only maintains market share, but seeks to be innovative as well, albeit not on the same scale as a prospector strategises. Most large companies fall into this category, as they seek to both protect their base of operations and generate new business opportunities.

Instead of seeking new growth opportunities and innovation, certain organisations follow a defender strategy, focusing on guarding their current markets, sustaining stable growth, and attending to current customers. *Defenders* are engineering-oriented and concentrate on preserving a secure niche in relatively unwavering market segments. Often a firm adopting a prospector strategy may oscillate to a defender strategy. This may happen when the firm effectively creates a new market and then endeavours to protect its market from competition.

DOI: 10.4324/9781003191384-6

According to Miles and Snow (1978), an organisation that pursues a *Reactor* strategy has no regular strategic approach; it floats through the tumultuous currents of environmental events. Drifting through the vicissitudes of time, it only reacts to, but fails to anticipate or impact those events. Generally, these organisations do not perform on the same scale as organisations that implement prospector, defender or analyser strategies.

Prospectors use a first-to-market strategy and typically succeed by being able to develop new technologies, products and markets rapidly (Conant, Mokwa, & Varadarajan, 1990; McDaniel & Kolari, 1987). Walker, Boyd, Mullins, and Larreche (2003) observed that prospectors require strength in research and development (R&D) of products and product engineering and perform best when the amount spent on product R&D is high. They also rely on solid market research and build close ties with distribution channels to ensure that the R&D produces products that meet customers' needs (Hambrick, 1983; McDaniel & Kolari, 1987; Shortell & Zajac, 1990). Ballas and Demirakos (2018) classified a host of R&D-intensive industries, in which prospector strategy execution adds substantial value to the shareholders' wealth and specifically identified such industries as in electronics and electrical equipment, pharmaceuticals and biotechnology and technology hardware and equipment sectors. IT capabilities enable internal communication and functional integration so critical to new product success (Bharadwaj, A. S., Bharadwaj, S. G., & Konsynski, 1999; Griffin & Hauser, 1996; Moenaert & Souder, 1996; Swanson, 1994). Further, HR in a prospector strategy is required to ensure composite coordination and communication mechanisms, as they must continually innovate for new product development to sustain market competitiveness (Robinson, Fornell, & Sullivan, 1992).

In contrast, defenders look for and maintain a secure niche in a relatively stable product or service segment. They do not vie for opportunities beyond their established product-market domain (McDaniel & Kolari, 1987; Shortell & Zajac, 1990). They tend to offer a comparatively limited range of products or services than their competitors and seek to protect their turfs by proffering higher quality, superior service and lower prices (Hambrick, 1983). Clearly, for achieving these objectives, HR in a defender strategy needs to create a high level of marketing and market-linking capabilities (Conant et al., 1990; Walker et al., 2003), and must focus on resource optimisation, cost-cutting and process developments.

A study by Yuan, Lu, Tian, and Yu (2020) depicts that firms following a prospector strategy are associated with better Corporate Social Responsibility (CSR) initiatives than those following a defender strategy. Specifically, compared with defenders, prospectors engage in more socially responsible behaviour, fewer socially irresponsible activities and perform better in both stakeholder- and third party-related CSR domains. Prospectors seek to take benefit of CSR, as their innovation-oriented strategy allows them not only to benefit more from CSR, but also to have more tolerance for the uncertainty, risk and long time horizon, linked to CSR engagement.

From Electrical and Automation Business of L&T to E&A, Schneider Electric India Pvt. Ltd.

One of the most profound innovations of mankind has been the generation of electricity. Access to electricity has lit up many villages, towns and districts; made young underprivileged students empowered enough to pursue their education; made people prosper through their small businesses they can run because of electricity. Thus, it has been critical for mitigation of poverty, economic growth and improvement of living standards. Yet, in today's world, there remains a huge gap between the people who get this basic necessity and the ones who cannot and around two billion people are still devoid of access to reliable energy, which blocks them from having a safe and decent life. This gap has been ever accentuating further, because of the digital divide. When the thinking population in the world is trying to decrease this gap by inclusion of everybody under the necessities of life, the world is faced with one of the biggest challenges, which is that of the climate change. After years of low cognizance and sluggish advancement, there is now wide-ranging recognition that the earth is on a critical climate trajectory. Fighting climate change requires redefining the energy model. Certain organisations, such as Schneider Electric (SE), believe that an all-digital, all-electric world can drive an entirely new level of efficiency and sustainability.

Schneider Electric is a French multinational company provisioning energy and automation digital solutions and its mission and vision are anchored into being a global specialist in energy management. For this reason, they want to help people develop products and systems for energy efficiency so that they can do more while using less resources from the planet. The company operates in more than 100 countries and engages over 135,000 people. Its strategy is to bring the worlds of energy and automation together in order to accomplish a high level of efficacy by designing and working on both the systems in simultaneity.

Schneider Electric was born during the first Industrial Revolution, when the Schneider Brothers acquired mines and forges at Le Creusot, France, in 1936 and 2 years later created Schneider & Cie. Beginning in steel, the company grew through enduring electrical distribution expertise. It undertook multiple strategic acquisitions since 2003, and today it is a global leader providing energy and automation digital solutions for efficiency and sustainability. At Schneider, this is called "Life Is On". SE believes that access to energy and digital is a basic human right and that the current generation is facing a revolutionary shift in energy transition and industrial revolution propelled by augmented digitisation in an increasingly electric world.

SE had humble beginnings in electrical industry, and when started its business, the only products it had were the ones that could be used as components to low voltage electrical installations. However, the company grew from strength to strength through expansion, restructuring and strategic acquisitions. SE combines energy with automation to achieve greater efficiency, built on real-time operational insights bringing in not only visibility and control of energy consumption for unceasing improvement and energy savings, but efficiencies in equipment and production as well. In the last two decades, SE has made extraordinary innovations that focus on connecting stand-alone devices in the Internet of Things (IoT) platform for energy efficiency solutions. A secure end-point to cloud ecosystem has been brought about through the conjunction of the IoT, big data and Artificial Intelligence from sensor to the cloud, which fosters total digital transparency as the same information is made available to not only the operators on the shop floor, but the C-suite as well. SE believes in full lifecycle management from design and build to operate and maintain through the power of end-to-end software with the same data model being utilised for both long-term operational performance and reduced costs as well as for augmenting efficiency in manufacturing and construction. These result in an ability to shift from site-by-site management to an integrated company management and helps consolidate energy and resource usage across the organisation to usher in a new level of competitiveness and efficiency.

SE is one of the first companies which determinedly pursued connecting anything possible within the electrical system to bring in energy efficiency. Their innovation of EcoStruxure is a blue ocean in energy management solutions that integrates multiple aspects and fosters energy efficiency and delivers a managerial tool for facilitating decision-making processes. EcoStruxure Power is an architecture that assimilates power management with business and industrial processes, IT services, building management and security management, and thus puts these into one platform delivering power in a safer, more reliable and more efficient manner.

Innovation and strategic acquisitions have been the core strengths of SE. In 1990s they acquired Clipsal of Australia, Square-D of USA and Telemecanique of France which formed the foundation of core products of SE. SE pursued its core expertise in electrical distribution by building on its Merlin Gerin and Square D brands. It acquired Clipsal in 2003, OVA, Merten and GET in 2006 and Marisio and Wessen in 2008, which reinforced its low voltage portfolio on a global scale. Their presence in new economies was augmented through the acquisition of stake in Delixi in China in 2006, Conzerv

Systems in 2009 and Luminous Power Technologies between 2011 and 2017 in India, and Steck Group in Brazil in 2011. Through the acquisitions of MGE UPS in 2004, followed by the acquisition of American Power Conversion (APC) in 2007, Microsol Tecnologia in Brazil in 2009 and APW in India in 2011, SE became the world leader in critical power technologies. Its position in electrical distribution was further enhanced through acquisition of AREVA T&D's medium voltage distribution division in June 2010, Electroshield-T Samara in Russia, and Telvent, a Spanish software company, in 2011. SE further reinforced its industrial automation technologies through the acquisitions of Citect in 2006, RAM Industries in 2008, Cimac and SCADA group in 2010 and Leader & Harvest in 2011. Its leadership in building automation was reinforced through the acquisition of Vizelia and D5X in 2010, Summit Energy in 2011, M&C Energy group in 2012 and IGE+XAO in 2018.

SE is also a research company that is investing EUR10 billion in innovation and research and development for sustainable development between 2015 and 2025. The company holds 20,000 patents either active or in application worldwide and invests 5% of its annual revenue in research and development. Looking ahead, with SE innovation in energy management solution, they are now in the frontline in aiming to have a carbon-neutral future by 2050.

In 2018, SE had announced its acquisition of L&T Electrical and Automation business, which it completed in 2020, making India to be its third-largest revenue market. As a process of this acquisition, SE owns a 65% stake in the business and global investment company Temasek owns the rest and a new entity – Schneider Electric India Private Limited (SEIPL) – is formed. In this newly formed entity, over 2,000 of Schneider Electric's pre-existing employees are joined in over by 5,000 employees from L&T's electrical and automation business from its markets in the Middle East, Africa, Indonesia and Malaysia. L&T's E&A business had a range of low- and medium-voltage switchgear, electrical systems, industrial and building automation solutions, energy management systems, metering solutions and projects and services business that are transferred to SE. The manufacturing facilities of E&A in Navi Mumbai, Ahmednagar, Vadodara, Coimbatore and Mysuru in India and related subsidiaries in UAE, Kuwait, Malaysia and Indonesia are also transferred to SE.

"This newly merged company will serve the priorities of India: Make in India for India and the rest of the world, Digital India, Skill India, Sustainable Energy, Smart Cities and Infrastructure for self-reliance, to bring tremendous value to our customers and stakeholders, employees, partners, suppliers, and community in which the company develops", said Jean-Pascal Tricoire, Chairman & CEO, Schneider Electric (L&T Sells its Electrical and Automation Business, 2020).

Exit from the electrical and automation business was a part of the strategic portfolio review process of L&T. "The closure of divestment of the E&A

business is a key milestone in our stated long-term strategy. The challenge was to carve out a business of this scale, with minimum disruption to the sprawling customer base and do it all amid the constraints of a pandemic", AM Naik, Group Chairman, Larsen & Toubro said. "We believe Schneider Electric is the right partner to grow the business, that L&T had nurtured and grown over decades. We truly believe that this deal with Schneider Electric is a win-win for our employees, business partners, and shareholders" (Thomas, 2020).

The Electrical and Automation business – the business that L&T had nurtured and grown over decades – had always been faced with a continuous challenge to sustain its leadership place through constant innovation and new product development. In order to help meet this challenge, it continually invested in research and development to evolve, progress and grow, while simultaneously it kept on capturing experiences and best practices. According to Mr. PK Bajaj, the then executive vice-president, L&T (Electrical & Automation), the firm had introduced products, which had sensors that talk to each other, or the IoT products that help organisations manage their power infrastructure better (as cited in Krishnan, 2016). "These are soft products which link up all the switches and boards. You can remotely look at load management in factory or manage switches if the MCB trips. The aim is to empower the customer to derive efficiency and safety", he said (as cited in Krishnan, 2016).

A continuous challenge for L&T (E&A) was to sustain its leadership place through constant innovation and new product development. In order to help meet this challenge, it used to invest in research and development to evolve, progress and grow, while simultaneously it keeps on capturing experiences and best practices. L&T E&A's consistent approach to innovation of products and processes, adoption of new technology, scouting for new businesses and new markets – all pointed to the organisation adopting a consistent prospector strategy. Almost the same characteristics of organisational strategy of research and innovation of SE led to the conclusion that SE was the right partner to grow the business. The Human Resources Department of E&A had built up its commensurate HR strategy supportive of a prospector strategy. This case study specifically examines a few strategic HR interventions undertaken by HR of L&T E&A to scrutinise and examine this proposition. In order to put things in perspective, the financials of L&T Electrical & Automation (E&A), as it existed, are depicted in Appendix 4.

Strategic Interventions in HR

L&T – E&A was a heritage organisation that had a 50-year history. The senior members in the organisation used to have a sense of pride and belongingness towards L&T. However, sometime in the early part of the last decade, it was observed that at the New Managerial Middle Management level, this sense of belongingness was declining. Formal and informal feedback from the employees demonstrated this largely. It was also evident from an Employee Survey carried out that many dimensions related to an engaged workforce showed a low score. These dimensions mostly included progress discussions, recognition, feeling of being cared for and development focus. Also, during discussions in various employee interaction forums, several connected issues emerged, such as:

a. Employees felt demotivated due to lack of appreciation. Timely feedback on their work was missing. Communication between managers and employees was weak. Developmental discussions never happened.
b. The managers, albeit technically very sound, were required to be sensitised towards their employees' needs. They had to be provided with adequate knowledge and understanding about handling teams.

These issues had a cascading effect on the individuals, teams, departments and organisation at large. Electrical and automation wanted to move towards a culture of better trust, recognition, openness, care, teamwork and thereby a better-engaged workforce. The organisation realised that two important areas that needed attention were focus on employee development by way of improving manager–employee relationship and creation of a platform of recognition. With these twin objectives, following two path-breaking initiatives were launched.

• Development program for Middle Managers titled "Creating Organisational Performance Excellence (COPE)".
• Reward and Recognition scheme.

Creating Organisational Performance Excellence (COPE)

The organisation identified a consultant, with whom this work could be carried out. The consultant was an experienced trainer in the field of leadership development, coaching and mentoring, assessment and feedback skills, competency building, high-impact communication and experiential learning. An in-depth analysis on the extant work environment was carried out through interactions with the business unit heads and through focus group discussions among the target employee population. The program was designed based on the findings to move towards a situational change.

The desired program outcome of COPE was identified as given herewith.

A   Mature and Evolved Managerial Cadre

People managers should understand their role as leaders and be committed to competencies such as team engagement, team development, mutual trust and open communication.

Energised and Engaged Teams

A few things that engage the Gen Y are – communication, feeling of being valued and clarity of role, a sense of growth by constantly having a development focus. Employees should be on a learning path that gives them exposure to newer challenges.

Culture of Recognition

Managers should be able to appreciate performance, understand the different motivational needs of team members and create a culture of recognition. "Pat on the back" attitude would infuse a lot of energy, drive, ownership and initiative in the work environment.

Capsule Design

Three contact points were envisaged in this journey of 6 months, an initiation workshop facilitated by the external consultant, coaching session of at least one hour with the participants of the workshop, or as often as the participants may seek, during the next six-month period and a Peer learning Workshop, which would mark a culmination of the programme.

The programmes in at least 5 days, spread over 6 months, were more of experiential learning through group activities and role plays. The initiation workshop consisted of 2 days of theoretical modules and a day's outbound activity. The focus areas during the initiation workshop were to inculcate the attributes portrayed herein.

My Team My Responsibility

Creating ownership, understanding the role of a team leader and key skills required in subordinates.

Dialoguing

Importance of dialogue in building rapport, creating genuine interest in the individual, show empathy, build trust and solve problems.

Creating a Development Focus

Assess employee potential, analyse the competency requirement of the role of the team member and identify gaps, create a Development Action plan for the employee to meet those requirements and review regularly.

Coaching and Feedback

In the context of McClleland's Needs theory, providing truthful and constructive feedback, gaining commitment.

At the end of the initiation workshop, every participant would take up a project which would essentially involve bringing in desired level of change in one or two of his/her team members, who had the potential to develop, but were not exhibiting desired levels of performance. The participant would work towards the development of the team member using the COPE constructs and towards self-development enhancing the key leadership skills.

One to One Coaching: 1 Hour

Even as the participants were free to interact and take support of the consultant at any time during the 60-day period of the programme after the workshop, a coaching contact of at least one hour during the 60-day period would necessarily take place which would help the participant to clarify issues and discuss about roadblocks that he/she might be facing. It would provide the necessary support for further smooth execution of the project.

High Impact Communication and Peer Learning Workshop: 2 Days

Finally, the program would culminate with a Peer Learning workshop where participants would share their success stories by making presentations. The project presentation would be evaluated by the peers and the facilitator. The evaluation forms would be shared with the participants. At the end, the best projects would be showcased to the senior management where the efforts of the participants would get recognised. Thus, it served as an opportunity for the participants to get useful feedback from the leadership.

With this design format, a clear linkage to the L&T competency framework was also established. The module proposed not only to enhance the current competencies, but also to develop competencies required for the next level in the leadership roles. Needless to mention that the role of firm strategic capabilities in creating economic value and sustaining competitive advantage has been greatly emphasised by researchers (Day, 1990).

The module was designed in such a way that it provided time to internalise the learning, convert it into action and evaluate its effectiveness. Further, it also implied a journey in continuity – the program might technically end post the Peer Learning workshop; however, participants would keep on applying the constructs with their teams. This allowed the individual to move up the four stages of competence learning, such as unconscious incompetence to conscious incompetence to conscious competence and finally unconscious competence.

Nominations and Communication

The key to success of a new HR initiative lies in its effective branding. The HR of L&T Electrical & Automation (E&A) took elaborate steps to announce the program, as portrayed herewith.

Working Out the Nominations

Functions and managers were identified who faced the issues of attrition and low-performance standards of employees. The intention was to target those areas where immediate attention was necessary.

Launching the Program

A detailed program document with the objective, learning outcome and facilitator profile was created.

Strategising the Communication

Personal communication/conversation was made with every Business Unit Head on the initiative followed by an email to confirm nominations.

Feedback

As a part of the closing session, HR captured participant feedback. The graph, as shown in Figure 5.1, captured the feedback on the program on a rating scale of 5. It clearly showed that consistently more than 90% of participants had given very positive feedback and had benefitted from the program. There was not even a single unfavourable response.

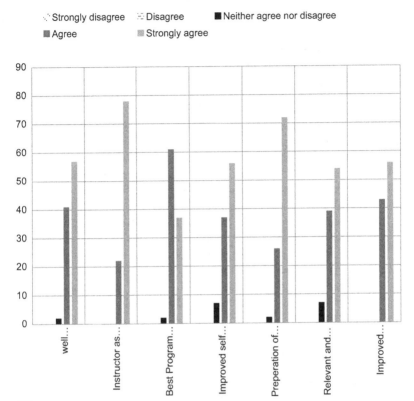

N.B:
1-Strongly disagree,
2-Disagree,
3- Neither agree nor disagree,
4-Agree,
5-Strongly agree

Figure 5.1 Feedback Scale on COPE

Participants' Responses

Undertaking a time-bound employee development project as a part of the program was for sure an innovative way of putting forward and ensuring the application of the learning. Participants showed dedication and genuine efforts to work with their identified project partners. A few best practices that were implemented by participants received appreciation from senior leadership, as mentioned herewith. These efforts went a long way in strengthening their teams.

> *Dialoguing.* Taking a genuine interest in employee development, discussion over a lunch/dinner outside of working hours, rapport building through dialogue about employees' family, hobbies and interests, showing empathy, etc. were manifestations of sound two-way communication implemented as best practices.
>
> *Skill Enhancement Through Development Action Plan (DAP).* Chalking out a documented DAP with timelines, regular review mechanism and strictly following the same, nominating employees for Technical and Behavioural training programs, encouraging them to take up Any Time Learning courses (L&T's internal web-based learning) were a few developmental initiatives.
>
> *Improve Employee Morale Through Appreciation.* Immediate appreciation for walking the extra mile, appreciating in a forum, writing congratulatory mails with senior leaders marked in copy and nominating them under rewards program were manifested as attempts at augmenting employee motivation.
>
> *Exposure.* Providing challenging work, enrich present roles and responsibilities, job rotations, reallocation of work, offloading certain non-value adding work were attempts at job enriching, aiming at intrinsic motivation.
>
> *Building Trust and Gaining Commitment.* Approach of "ask more and tell less", employee bound to think by themselves, introspect and come out with solutions, were strategies at developing team members. Thus, the team members gained commitment on the task, with 100% effort from the individual.
>
> *Change in Self Leadership Style.* The leadership development strategies adopted were doing away with the self-styled, Herculean approach, delegate responsibility, increase accountability, empower employees down the line, provide freedom of work, provide support when needed and appreciate from time to time, and so on.

Rewards and Recognition Scheme

Innovative, practical and workable rewards and recognition programs have become essential organisational tools for motivating employees in today's world (Shalini, 2020).

With the Employee Survey scores emerging in L&T (E&A), it was evident that having a structured Rewards and Recognition program in place was the need of the hour, as a Rewards scheme would not only improve the engagement level, but also bring more and best out of employees. HR of L&T E&A interacted with other companies into similar businesses, such as Honeywell, Siemens, Ericsson and Tata Power and with other businesses within L&T group such as L&T Infotech and L&T Hydrocarbon to study different Reward and Recognition initiatives. To build the program framework, a structured method was followed envisaging: understand practices followed in other L&T units as well as other companies; understand employee feedback; understand present practices within L&T E&A at different locations and obtain views of the senior leadership.

The observations emanating from this exercise, inter alia, were:

- A need for a common platform of appreciation was felt by employees;
- Recognition at L&T E&A was happening in different pockets and it needed to be standardised as well as expanded to reach all;
- The senior leadership suggested to encourage Team Awards to bring about a change from individualised working styles to a cohesively contributing team working style.

With this background, a detailed award scheme was designed keeping in mind the motivational needs of employees at various levels. The salient points of the scheme were as given herewith.

The purpose of the award scheme was to motivate employees to perform at higher levels and sustain excellence in performance, for achieving organisational goals, to create and encourage a team-based performance culture and to encourage employees to be innovative and undertake ground-breaking initiatives having a substantial positive impact on E&A's business.

The scheme covered all supervisory and above employees spread across locations in India, which implied a strength of around 3,000 employees, spread over 10 business units including sales and marketing teams.

Reward Categories

The Rewards and Recognition program at L&T (E&A) was two-tier in nature, with mechanisms and awards, existing at both the unit and organisation levels.

The details of the Structure of Reward and Recognition Programme at L&T (E&A) are given in Table 5.1.

The details of the frequency and salient points of various Reward and Recognition Programme at unit and organisation levels as it was designed and implemented are depicted in Appendix 6. In the reward system, apart from performance, innovation and teamwork, patents awards were

Table 5.1 Structure of Reward and Recognition Programme at L&T (E&A)

Unit Level Rewards	
Type	*Awards*
Individual Awards	E-Appreciation Awards (Individual)
	Star GET Award
	Star JET/DET Award
	Dronacharya Award
	Enlightener Award
Team Awards	E-Appreciation Awards (Team)
	Star Team Award
	Quantum Leap Project Award
Common Awards (Individual/Team)	Ground Breaker Innovation Award
	Humanitarian Champion Award
Organisation Level	
Team Awards	Ace Team Award
	Ace Project Award
	HR Excellence Award
Common Awards (Individual/Team)	Ace Innovation Award
	Ace Intellect Award
	Ace Publication Award

institutionalised to reward not only the internal trainers, but those who contribute largely to the society as well.

Online Platform – A Unique Feature of Rewards and Recognition

The most innovative feature of the process was its online platform which helped serve as a unique social and collaborative recognition platform, create excitement and buzz around rewards and recognition, and thus motivated all, especially the young workforce, and served as an end to end solution, with the power of social networking, along with the facility of interconnection with an online redemption store.

All information on the awards categories was provided on the e-platform. Employees could send out appreciation notes, wish birthdays and anniversaries, say "Thank you", etc., through the e-platform. It served as a very strong mechanism to quickly appreciate good work done and provided company-wide visibility.

Special Efforts Taken for Communication

The authorised policy document was circulated to all employees; however, certain additional methods were used to popularise this new scheme, viz. regular emails regarding online platform, posters on every floor and break-out areas, special communication drives at various manufacturing locations, and so on.

Administration of Awards

The Unit Level Awards were executed by the "Unit Level Rewards Committee" which was constituted for every business unit. The committee comprised Unit Head as the Chairman and three other senior persons, preferably of General Manager and above level rank, as members. The Unit HR Head/ Business HR partner acted as the convener of the committee. The committee met once in a quarter to scrutinise the quarterly applications and select the winners, based on the evaluation parameters. The winners were then announced by HR through email circulars.

Similarly, the Organisation Level Reward Committee comprised Business Head as the Chairman, Business Group Heads (Products and Projects Business) and Head-Finance as the members and HR Head as the convener of the committee.

E&A, SEIPL: Concluding Observations

According to Ghoshal (2003, p. 109), the basic proposition in Organisational Strategy Structure and Process (OSSP) is that "successful companies need to develop consistency among their strategy, the business model they adopt, including the choice of technology, and their organisational capability, including human resource practices". From the HR interventions depicted herewith, a few salient points emerge which clearly reflect the HR strategy typical to an organisation having prospector strategy. Prospectors generally have very elaborate internal communication mechanism and the same is true for L&T E&A, as depicted in Appendix 7. Prospectors put a great emphasis on organisational capability which is nothing but the summation of the competencies of the employees in the organisation. The twin interventions studied depict the great emphasis the organisation puts on behavioural competencies and the mechanisms required for reinforcing such competencies.

6 Critical Success Factors in ERP-SAP Implementation and HR

These days, volatile, uncertain and continuously evolving socioeconomic and political environments and public pressures propel governments to deliver effective and efficient public services. In order to meet such expectations, governments design extensive reforms, frame rigorous performance objectives and assiduously seek to implement them to improve the effectiveness and responsiveness of their agencies (Syed, Bandara, French, & Stewart, 2018). Nowadays public sector and Government organisations are also implementing ERP for information on real time and for having better administrative control (Nikookar, Safavi, Hakim, & Homayoun, 2010). Such organisations have greater social obligations, public answerability and distinctive culture (Anwar & Mohsin, 2011) and ERP helps them meet their requirements with precision.

Various vendors provide ERP solutions. However, the major ones are SAP, Microsoft Dynamic, Oracle, JDEdward and People-soft. Notwithstanding the benefits that accrue from a successful ERP implementation, there are indications of failure of projects on ERP implementations (Davenport, 1998). Hence, sound managerial principles suggest that there should be scrutiny of the Critical Success Factors (CSF) that impact such implementation and adherence to the CSFs through the phases of ERP implementation should be ensured.

Critical Success Factors, Change Management and ERP-SAP Implementation

CSFs have been one of the earliest and most actively researched topics (Lee & Ahn, 2008). CSFs encompass the internal and external stimuli that conditions change in organisations. These influence organisational vision and strategies, shape the long-term and short-term objectives of an organisation, tactical decision-making and evaluation of results. All these factors lead to adaption to change and ensure business success. Enterprise Resource Planning (ERP) is a highly popular change management tool. It has been resorted to by organisations world over to rationalise and integrate their processes.

DOI: 10.4324/9781003191384-7

The legacy systems were operating in stand-alone mode and hence ran to creation of silos. Such working led to problems of coordination and replication, and eventual delays in execution and dissatisfaction of stakeholders. Hence, ERP arose as a solution to seamlessly integrate things and make the processes smoother, faster, leaner and robust (Gunjal, 2019).

CSFs s were introduced by John F. Rockart and the MIT Sloan School of Management in 1979 in a way to help senior executives express their information needs for managing their organisations. Rockart (1979) traced his CSF work to its theoretical precursor, "success factors,", introduced by D. Ronald Daniel in 1961.

Daniel (1961) discussed the problem of scanty managerial data for setting objectives, determining strategies, taking decisions and determining results against objectives. Daniel (1961) also proclaimed that information for organisational strategy should focus on "success factors", which he described as "three to six factors that determine success. . . key jobs (that) must be done exceedingly well for a company to be successful". In a sequel, Rockart (1979) defined CSFs as a limited number of areas, in which results, if they are satisfactory, will guarantee successful competitive performance for the organisation. CSFs are thus the handful of crucial areas where an organisation must accomplish well regularly to actualise its vision.

Some key characteristics of CSFs are CSF hierarchy, types and stability over time.

Daniel (1961) described success factors at the industry level, which are shared across organisations inside the industry. Even as Daniel concentrated on ubiquitous, industry-level success factors (i.e., success factors applicable for any business in an industry), Anthony, Dearden, and Vancil (1972) expanded Daniel's work by suggesting that CSFs could differ within a company even from manager to manager, thereby elongating the concepts of managerial-level CSFs and organisationally unique CSFs.

Bullen and Rockart (1981) offered a thorough exposition of the hierarchical nature of CSFs and identified four levels: *industry, organisational, division* and *individual*. Caralli, Stevens, Willke, and Wilson (2004) drew an explicit parallel between CSF and planning hierarchy and pointed out that both hierarchies are interdependent. They summarised, however, that CSFs do not necessarily flow through the different strata of an organisation in simple one-to-one relationships.

Rockart identified five types of CSFs categorised with respect to the manner in which they add to the fructification of objectives:

i. The structure of the industry (*industry CSFs*);
ii. Competitive strategy, industry position and geographical location (*strategy CSFs*);
iii. The macroenvironment (*environmental CSFs*);

iv.   Problems or challenges to the organisation (*temporal CSFs*);
v.   Management perspective (*management CSFs*).

Although CSFs may remain static over time, CSFs change "as the industry's environment changes, as the company's position within an industry changes, or as particular problems or opportunities arise" (Bullen & Rockart, 1981).

In many changing organisations, CSFs remain of primordial importance because CSFs include all the internal and external influences that conditions change in organisations. External and internal factors such as technological, environmental, marketing and managerial, concomitantly affect the business model and generally constitute the CSFs in the organisation. In brief, the following five factors are the main determinants of CSFs that bring change.

i.   The environmental context: the forces of entrants, consumers, suppliers and competitors (Porter, 1985);
ii.   Marketing context: Product differentiation, cost, time of work, distribution and promotion (Porter, 1985);
iii. The managerial context: structure, systems, skills, style and staff (Damanpour, 1991; Kotter, 2008);
iv.   The organisational context: interfirm relationship and the competence level (Gates, 2010);
v.   Technological context: facility and necessity of use (Gates, 2010).

These five factors are mostly responsible for setting the objectives, shaping the strategies, taking decisions and measuring results, which eventually lead to adapt to change and achieve success in business.

Notwithstanding the benefits which accrue from a successful ERP implementation, there are indications of failure of projects on ERP implementations (Davenport, 1998). Or rather there is a high-risk propensity towards failure (Chatzoglou, P., Fragidis, Chatzoudes, D., & Symeonidis, 2016). Hence, it is sensible to scrutinise the CSFs that impact the success of such implementations. The identification, explanation and communication of CSFs help the team sustain its concentration on important aspects of the project and avoid outlay on less important parts (Tsiga, Emes, & Smith, 2016).

A clear understanding of the goals and objectives for which the ERP system is being implemented is emphasised as a CSF by researchers. It is said that the enterprise needs to define with clarity the objective of ERP system implementation with respect to its business needs (Krupp, 1998; Latamore, 1999; Santos, Santana, & Elhimas, 2018; Schragenheim, 2000; Travis, 1999).

Many point out that commitment of and participation by top management is an absolute necessity for ERP implementation (Chausi, B. A., Chausi, A., & Dika, 2016; Davis & Wilder, 1998; Laughlin, 1999; Oden, Langenwalter, & Lucier, 1993; Sherrard, 1998). It is necessary that the execution project should have an executive management planning committee dedicated to enterprise integration. The committee should understand ERP, provision the expenses, ask for returns and support the project. Besides, the project needs to be headed by an esteemed, managerial-level project champion (Krupp, 1998; Maxwell, 1999; Santos et al., 2018). The implementation should be riveted on and be directed by the requirements of business and not of the IT department (Chew, Leonard-Barton, & Bohn, 1991; Minahan, 1998).

The committee should be supported by a great ERP implementation team, which should consist of able and efficient resources, selected for their competencies, track records, peerless reputation, and flexibility and should be delegated with commensurate decision-making obligations (Chausi, B. A., Chausi, A., & Dika, 2016; Davis & Wilder, 1998; Laughlin, 1999; Minahan, 1998; Sherrard, 1998). There should be incessant communication with this team; however, the team should be vested with rapid decision-making ability (Sherrard, 1998). It is said that ERP implementation requires unflinching commitment by all people involved, from the top management to the lower management (Peterson, Gelman, & Cooke, 2001).

World-class project management, encompassing clarity of objectives, well-spelt-out work plan and resource plan and a schedule for assiduous tracking of progress of project (Davis & Wilder, 1998; Laughlin, 1999; Santos et al., 2018; Sherrard, 1998) is an essential CSF. Further, the project plan should be aggressive, albeit achievable, and should infuse and uphold a critical sense of urgency (Laughlin, 1999). It is essential that both the consultant and the client should work on agreed-upon strategy and project plan, and this would play a crucial role for ERP success (Mohamed, 1995).

ERP implementation is a gigantic exercise in organisational transformation and ushers in enormous changes encompassing diverse aspects of organisational life (Al-Mashari, 2003; Chausi, B. A., Chausi, A., & Dika, 2016). The organisational change management issues concomitant to ERP implementation are segmented by Edwards and Humphries (2005) into "communications and relationships" and "understanding the business". There is no gainsaying that people as well as their communications and interfaces change through ERP implementation. Generally, management adopts change management strategy taking cognizance of users' needs and reasons for resistance and uses strategy to tide over the critical issues and evaluates the status of the management efforts (Aladwani, 2001).

Employees' understanding of the usage of the ERP is another impediment in ERP implementation (Aladwani, 2001; Kraemmergaard & Rose, 2002).

The new ERP necessitates a transition in the work behaviour of employees and this could raise resistance. Egan and Fjermestad (2005) aver that resistance is largely because of lack of skill or understanding of the change that come about by the ERP process. Many have approached change management by using the rudimentary attitude to behaviour (A!B) model (Ajzen & Fishbein, 1980), which suggests that for changing behaviour, a change in attitudes is essential and once attitudes change, it directly results in a change in behaviour.

Generally, management adopts change management strategy taking cognizance of users' needs and reasons for resistance and uses strategy to tide over the critical issues and evaluates status of the management efforts (Aladwani, 2001).

With the help of the tool of CSFs, many facets of information systems and ERP systems implementations have been scrutinised (Bancroft, Seip, & Sprengel, 1998; Clemons, 1998; Dolmetsch, Huber, Fleisch, & Österle, 1998; Holland, Light, & Gibson, 1999; Kale, 2000; Parr, Shanks, &Darke, 1999;Santos et al., 2018; Stefanou, 1999; Sumner, 1999).

Providing training in new skills or giving employees time after a demanding period (Aladwani, 2001) are some of the approaches through which resistance is sought to be overcome. It has been advocated that setting aside 10–15% of the entire ERP execution budget for training will give an enterprise 80% chance of implementation success (McCaskey & Okrent, 1999; Volwer, 1999). Widespread education and training are generally taken as a CSF (Chausi, B. A., Chausi, A., & Dika, 2016).

Avoidance of customisation is taken as another CSF. It is said that organisation should avoid unnecessary customisation (Rothenberger & Srite, 2009) for the success of ERP implementation. If it is decided to implement a regular ERP package without much customisation, the need to customise the basic ERP code will be reduced, which will moderate project complexities and facilitate keeping the schedule of implementation on track (Sherrard, 1998).

Accuracy of data entered and adopting accurate data entry techniques are considered as critical factors. Since ERP consists of integrated and interrelated processes, if wrong data are entered, it has a cascading effect, which affects many other related processes all through the company. Hence, the importance attached to data accuracy and accuracy of data entry techniques is considered a CSF in an ERP implementation (Chausi, B. A., Chausi, A., & Dika, 2016; Santos et al., 2018; Stedman, 1999; Stein, 1999). Further, it is essential that all archaic and informal systems must be eliminated. Else, some staff may prefer to use the old, archaic systems (Hutchins, 1998).

Esteves and Pastor-Collado (2000) collated the CSFs prevailing in ERP literature, examined the similarities between them and unified the motley lists of CSFs to shape those into an integrated CSFs model. They categorised the CSFs into four perspectives: strategic, tactical, organisational and technological. The strategic perspective relates to the core competencies considered essential for actualisation of the organisational vision and mission, while the tactical one to the realisation of business objectives with short-term timelines. The organisational perspective, which is concerned with overarchic organisation-level issues such as structure, culture and business, is considered more important than technological perspective, which rivets on technical aspects, such as hardware and base software needs, and the particular ERP product in consideration, and so on. Thus, the CSFs which are both organisational and strategic are sustained management support, effective organisational change management, adequate project team composition, good project scope management, comprehensive business re-engineering, adequate project champion role, trust between partners and user involvement and participation. The ones that are organisational, but tactical are dedicated staff and consultants, appropriate usage of consultants, empowered decision makers, adequate training program, strong communication inwards and outwards, formalised project plan/schedule and reduce trouble shooting. There are three CSFs that are considered strategic and technological viz. avoid customisation, adequate ERP implementation strategy and adequate ERP version, as against two which are tactical and technological, such as adequate software configuration and adequate legacy systems knowledge.

As is evident, even though Human Resource Management per se has not been characterised as a CSF, HR department invariably is the process owner of several CSFs, viz. Effective Organisational Change, User involvement and participation, Trust between Partners, Dedicated Staff and Consultants and Strong Communications Inward and Outwards, Adequate Training Program.

One of the critical issues in SAP research is the management of CSFs in SAP implementations. CSFs play varying importance during the various phases of SAP implementation project. CSFs are not, per se, directly manageable. Rather, management directly owns, defines measures and manages the processes along different phases of SAP implementation. Hence, there is a need to relate the CSFs to the phase-wise ASAP project implementation processes to understand the relative importance of the CSFs during the different phases of Accelerated SAP (ASAP) implementations.

In 1996, SAP introduced the ASAP implementation methodology for augmenting the speed of SAP implementation projects. Since, the first author of the book functioned as the Head of HR of the instant subject company when the research was carried out, participant observation as a methodology of data collection was an inescapable necessity in this case study. Schensul, S.L., Schensul, J.J., and LeCompte, M.D. (1999) defined participant observation as "the process of learning through exposure to or involvement in the day-to-day or routine activities of participants in the researcher setting" (p. 91).

Esteves and Pastor-Collado (2001) offer a theoretical model to establish the relationship of CSFs vis-à-vis Accelerated SAP (ASAP) processes along with an assessment of their relevance across the ASAP phases. The case examines how the results of Esteves and Pastor-Collado (2001) have been utilised in OPGC ASAP implementation and HR's role in it.

OPGC: A Story of Transitions

Odisha Power Generation Corporation Limited (OPGC) was incorporated in 1984. OPGC started as a wholly owned government company of the State of Odisha with the main objective of establishing, operating and maintaining large thermal power generating stations. It set up two thermal power plants with a capacity of 210 MW each in the IB valley area of Jharsuguda District in the State of Odisha (Ib Thermal power Station), in 1994 and 1996, respectively. Later, in 1999, as part of Power Sector Reforms, 49% equity was disinvested in favour of AES through a process of international competitive bidding and a balance 51% continued to be held by the Government of Odisha. The day-to-day management was vested with the nominee of strategic investor AES. The Board of Directors consisted of six members, three each from Government and AES. Out of three Functional Directors, Director Finance was nominated by the Government of Odisha and Managing Director and Director Operation from AES. As 51% shareholding was with the Government of Odisha, the company continued to be considered as a government company within the meaning of the Companies Act. OPGC was subject to audit by Controller and Auditor General under Companies Act. At the same time post reforms and disinvestment, OPGC introduced several good practices and rewards system in the organisation, which were otherwise not prevalent in the state sector PSUs. Variable Pay Plan, Market Salary Structure, Project roll employment, 360-degree appraisal, balanced scorecard and team building interventions were some such practices. Also, OPGC was the only state PSU wherein disinvestment of this magnitude with divesting of day-to-day management to strategic investor took place. Thus, OPGC, albeit a state PSU group, had a different footing.

OPGC set up two supercritical units of 660 MW each and both units achieved commercial operation date (COD) in July 2019 and August 2019, respectively. As a part of its global strategy to reduce carbon footprint from its portfolio, AES Corporation decided to exit OPGC and inked share sale and purchase agreement (SSPA) with Adani Power for sell of its 49% equity in OPGC. Earlier AES had declared its goal to reduce its generation from coal to below 30% by the end of 2020 and to less than 10% by the end of 2030 (Adani to acquire, 2020). In a complete reversal of its privatisation policy, the Government of Odisha decided to exercise its right of first refusal (RoFR) to buy out 49% equity stake (Odisha nixes Adani Plan, 2020). Accordingly, AES transferred its stake of 49% equity to Odisha Hydro Power Corporation (OHPC), the agency authorised by the Odisha government and the sale and purchase agreement (SSPA) with Adani Power was cancelled. Thus, OPGC became a fully owned company of the Government of Odisha with effect from 10 December 2020.

The vision, mission and core values of the company were adopted through a bottom-up approach in 2011. A nationally acclaimed Corporate Trainer and HR consultant had been engaged as an external facilitator for crafting the vision and mission and adopting the core values of OPGC. The said consultant conducted a series of workshops with a broad subset of OPGC employees on vision, mission and values with the broad objective of clearly understanding the views of representative sample of OPGC employees on it and of collating and summarising information and data. Finally, at an apex level workshop, where the entire leadership team of OPGC, participated, the Vision, Mission and Values for OPGC were crafted through a participatory and consensual approach. The vision statement adopted was "A world-class power utility committed to generate clean, safe and reliable power, enhancing value for all stake holders and contributing to national growth". The mission statement consisted of three elements viz. to attain global best practices by adopting, innovating and deploying cutting edge solutions, to achieve excellence in reliability, safety and quality of power, by creating a culture of empowerment and high performance and to be a responsible corporate citizen having concern for environment, society, employees and people at large. The company also adopted six core values viz. Put Safety First, Honour our commitments, Act with integrity, Strive for Excellence, Have Organisational Pride and Foster Teamwork.

The progression of revenue and profit after tax of OPGC are depicted in Appendix 4.

ASAP Implementation: Benefits, Phases and Strategy

OPGC embarked on an IT transformation journey in 2015 by implementing SAP solution for Energy business. The SAP led business transformation exercise was undertaken through the business partner Accenture and was carried out across the following critical business processes:

a. HR and Pay Roll (HR);
b. Finance and Controlling (FICO);
c. Procurement & Material Management (MM);
d. Asset and work management (PM/WCM);
e. Environment Health and Safety (EHS);
f. Project Systems (PS).

The objective of this initiative was to achieve and sustain SAP-led business excellence through:

a. Common business processes aligned to strategic objectives of OPGC;
b. Standardised business systems and applications;
c. Accurate and timely business data and MIS;
d. Processes aligned to leading practices;
e. Implement applicable SAP functionalities.

The Project kick-off was done on 23rd March 2015 and Go Live was carried out on 1 February 2016. Accenture utilised its proprietary Accenture Delivery Management methodology for the successful execution of the OPGC Accelerated SAP implementation project. SAP Initiative in OPGC took 10 months to deploy, and 4 months of Post Go Live Support.

Benefits of the IT Intervention

The key elements and benefits targeted by the SAP Rollout Implementation are presented herewith:

Business Improvisation

*   Reduction in administrative overhead through the simplification of processes;
*   Allowing staff to focus on analysis rather than transactional issues;
*   Empowerment to end users;
*   Better decisions due to better access of information;
*   System-enabled monitoring and control of processes in line with ISO Standards;
*   Controlled expenditure of projects and procurement through system-driven budgetary controls;
*   Optimised inventory levels and procurement efficiency;
*   Reconciliation and tracking of material issued to contractor;

- Effective management of vendor database focusing on rewarding the high performing vendors through vendor rating;
- System capable of generating effective management reporting;
- One A/c process one GL;
- Centralisation of processes for efficiency;
- Better financial control due on online update;
- Standardisation of Country – India-specific tax and accounting processes.

IT Systems Rationalisation

- One IT system and landscape;
- Centralised management;
- Extensible architecture.

System and Process Optimisation

- One centre responsible for information system;
- Guided and not forced implementation;
- Meeting Legal requirements for country India.

The Phases of ASAP Implementation

Figure 6.1 provides the details of the activities that were executed phase-wise throughout the Project implementation lifecycle.

Process-Wise Activities Vis-à-Vis the Management of the CSFs

The ASAP processes having been delineated, HR and SAP implementation team focused on identifying which CSF must be taken care of while implementing the specific ASAP processes, as per the five-phase paradigm. The CSFs which emerged as the most important ones having largest number of occurrences across the CSF implementation were Project Champion's role, sustained management support and user involvement and participation. Based on the findings, the SAP governance plan was accordingly customised. The Steering Committee consisting of Managing Director, all Functional Directors, OPGC Project Manager, and external Consultant met every month. Similarly, Weekly Review Meetings of OPGC Project Manager, OPGC Core Team, OPGC Business Process Owners along with Project Manager and Project Leads were carried out. Fortnightly Business Process Owners Meetings and Weekly Module Level Meetings were also envisaged for augmenting user involvement and participation.

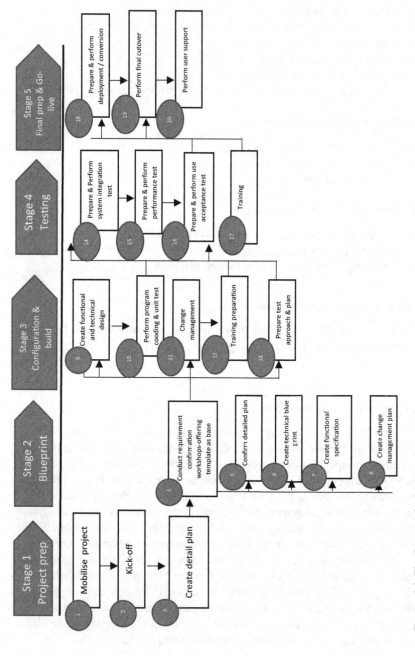

Figure 6.1 The Stages of ASAP Implementation

CSFs' Relevance Vis-à-Vis the Phase-Wise ASAP Processes

Then, the relevance of each CSF in each phase of ASAP implementation was ascertained through cross-comparison method. The views of important stakeholders with respect to CSF's relevance in each phase of implementation were ascertained on a scale of High, Normal and Low. These views were examined, compared, both with respect to within OPGC functions as well as vis-à-vis Accenture and also with respect to Esteves and Pastor-Collado (2000) model and analysis of reasonings as to the variations in perceptions was ascertained. The collated information is depicted in Appendix 8.

A summary of the CSFs ratings (i.e., the Overall ratings) of all OPGC leads (both HR and Non-HR) in terms of relevance of the CSF in an identifiable phase is given in Table 6.1.

As can be seen from Table 6.1, in Phase 1, nine CSFs were rated as of high relevance. Similarly, in Phase 2, 13 CSFs, in phase 3, eight CSFs, in Phase 4, seven CSFs and in Phase 5 five CSFs, were considered highly relevant by the stakeholders. The strategy in OPGC was to give greater focus on the highly relevant CSFs phase-wise until the implementation was taken to logical conclusion.

OPGC: Concluding Observations

The study aims to customise the Esteves and Pastor-Collado (2001) Model of relevance of CSFs in ERP-SAP Implementation to the specific conditions of OPGC. The study, apart from being a part of the research by the first author, was, in fact, a part of the implementation process in OPGC. The study equipped the OPGC members with knowledge as to relevance of each CSF in each of the ASAP implementation process and thus helped monitor the implementation. It is important that the practitioners of SAP implementation need to customise the model as to the specific requirements of the organisation. All said, there is no gainsaying that knowledge and customisation of the model would go a long way in SAP implementation in any organisation, which is considered as a major change management initiative in any organisation these days.

Further, this case study is a way forward in substantive theory building in the matter of relevance of CSFs in implementation of ERP-SAP. In the process, the model also gets validated in different situations (Mishra, Shukla, & Sujatha, 2019b). Substantive theory gets built in the framework of finding differences and similarities of contextualised occurrences, and designs, across and within case studies engrossed on analogous themes. A revalidated substantive theory is all the more transferable, albeit not

Table 6.1 Phase-Wise Ratings of Relevance of CSFs in OPGC

CSF Relevance along the ASAP Implementation Phases		Phase 1 (Project Preparation)	Phase 2 (Business Blueprinting)	Phase 3 (Business Realisation)	Phase 4 (Final Preparation)	Phase 5 (Go Live & Support)
		Overall Rating	Overall Rating	Overall Rating	Overall Rating	Overall Rating
Organisational Perspective	Sustained Management Support	High	High	High	Normal	High
	Effective Organisational Change	Normal	Normal	Normal	Normal	Normal
	Good Project Scope Management	Normal	High	High	Normal	Normal
	Adequate Project Team Composition	High	High	Normal	Normal	Normal
	Meaningful Business Process Reengineering	Normal	High	Normal	Normal	Normal
	User involvement and participation	Normal	High	High	Normal	High
	Project Champion Role	Normal	High	Normal	High	High
	Trust between Partners	High	High	High	High	Normal
	Dedicated Staff and Consultants	High	High	High	High	High

	High	High	High	High	High	High
Strong communications inward and outwards	High	High	High	High	High	High
Formalised Project plan/schedule	High	High	High	Normal	Normal	Normal
Adequate training program	Normal	Normal	Normal	Normal	High	Normal
Preventive troubleshooting	Normal	Normal	Normal	Normal	High	Normal
Usage of appropriate consultant	High	High	High	High	High	Normal
Adequate ERP implementation strategy	High	High	Normal	Normal	Normal	Normal
Technical perspective — Avoid customisation	Normal	Normal	Normal	Normal	Normal	Normal
Adequate ERP version	Normal	Normal	Normal	Normal	Normal	Normal
Adequate software configuration	Normal	Normal	High	High	Normal	Normal
Adequate legacy system knowledge	High	High	High	Normal	Normal	Normal

generalisable, in the sense that elements of the context can be superimposed on contexts with similar features to the context under study. Theory building requires continual comparison of data and theory (Glaser & Strauss, 1967) and an incessant refinement between theory and practice (Lynham, 2000).

Conclusions

The book has taken up six case studies on six distinct dimensions of the research topic. All the six dimensions, taken up in the case studies are highly relevant and significant for the contemporaneity of the themes. Also, as significant is the brand value of these case companies, as the contemporaneity of the themes.

Summary

The book studies the role of HR in six different contexts and six different dimensions. Learnings from case studies highlight that HR plays an important role in organisation's change process. Such role includes designing and implementing Organisation Development strategies, change interventions and functional level HPWPs. It involves developing the training programs related to the change, assessing organisational readiness for change, developing timelines, communicating such strategies, building rewards systems to maintain and reinforce change, obtaining feedback from the employees during the change process in the organisation and supporting new behaviours to keep the firm competitive, and the like. No two cases use same set of variables manifest as HRM practices in the six cases studied. The intention of the study has not been to build a comparison of common variables in different companies, but to carry out the objectives of the study in variegated dimensions and make the research holistic.

The Case 'Global Efficiencies Through Local Practices' takes up the issue of HR's role in the context of the organisational strategy of leveraging on the global support systems of DHL, while continuing with the robust business practices prevalent in the local conditions. Duly supported by HR, Blue Dart has built its leadership pipeline through home-grown talent for which majority of the leadership roles in Blue Dart India, such as, Managing Director, Finance Director, Chief Operating Officer, Customer Service Head, Air OPS Head, all Regional and Sales Heads and IT heads have

DOI: 10.4324/9781003191384-8

grown internally through the ranks of Blue Dart India. In HR, the policies, systems and practices of Blue Dart are primarily India-centric catering to the local requirements. However, the best practices prevalent in DHL at the global level such as the Employee of the Year (EOY) award, certification as specialists Programme and Motiv8 framework are adopted in India. Blue Dart is an ideal example of a multinational company where global efficiencies are achieved largely through local practices (Mishra et al., 2018).

In the case of "Transformational Journey of an Indian 'Maharatna' Company", the case demonstrates how HR reoriented itself, when NTPC lifted itself on the growth path and altered its very name from National Thermal Power Corporation to NTPC Limited on 28 October 2005, to reflect the diversification of NTPC's business operations beyond thermal power generation to include, among others, generation of power from hydro, nuclear and renewable energy sources and undertaking coal mining and oil exploration activities. The case also shows how Human Resource Strategy, while continuing on the erstwhile four-dimensional paradigm of building competence, building commitment, building systems and building culture, was to form a very important segment on which the entire organisational transformation strategy was to rivet.

NTPC case is a historical case study. Arnold (2000) suggests that "all history in some way wishes to say something about its own present time" and the need is "to interpret the past, not simply present it". This case depicts how the basic tenets of the HR strategy in its four Building Blocks of Competency, Commitment, Culture and Systems Building had to undergo changes so that the HR function supported the Organisational Transformation NTPC was undergoing during this period. The true value of historiographic research lies in ensuring that the readers build such analogies about things as are correct. Nibbling through history is a manifestation of an incessant search for patterns and attempt to learn how such patterns can be duplicated from one situation to another through the evolution of time. This study presents substantial connections among phenomena to serve as an aid to understand the role of HR in organisational transformation.

In the chapter "Professionalisation of Family Business", the case depicts how HR, vested with inculcating the desired culture within the organisation, has supported the company to bring about the organisational transformation on the journey of professionalism. Professionalisation of a family business is a journey from pure family firms to organisations managed through and by professionals. Family businesses as they traverse through time find themselves at different levels of professionalisation. HR becomes one of the initial functions to transform and bring about the organisational transformation on the journey of professionalism. It is perceived that the professionalisation of HR as a function involves setting up common standards of entry, performance and exits, known and standardised processes of codes of conduct and dealing with breaches thereof, benchmarked best practices regarding structures, systems and processes, definition and gaining of requisite levels of competencies, and the like. To prop up the organisational transitioning process in JSPL in 2007 and 2010, appropriate HR systems and processes have been sought to be designed in the Project Drishti and Project Nav Tarang, and JSPL HR has played its role in bringing about the desired changes and professionalism in the company to meet the requirements of business.

In the chapter "Changing Contours of Unionism and HR as an Enabler", the case depicts HR's role in one of the most contentious areas, such as, industrial relations. Participative Management is one of the High Performing Work Practices (HPWPs) being pursued in many of the organisations in modern days. Even as the Participative Management is a generic term involving participation of all sections of employees, viz. executives and non-executives, in India in the context of Employee Relations, it is specifically used as Workers' Participation in Management. Trade Unions are perceived as an important instrumentality for creating efficacious situations leading to successful participatory management. Diverse situational factors of current-day business scenarios have converged to bring in transition of the roles of trade unions from primarily bargaining institutions to specialised organisations focused on representing the interests of labour for betterment of QWL. Trade unions at NALCO are as much involved in improving the QWL of employees, as in maintaining good industrial relations. Roles that have earlier been considered as secondary ones with respect to Unions have eclipsed the earlier roles of collective bargaining and instead have metamorphosed them as watchdogs of welfare measures and QWL. Partnering in the day-to-day activities in the organisation not only through Participatory Fora, but through the implementation of the communication matrix, pitchforks the Unions into their new role of 'Partners in Progress'. HR can and does facilitate this transition by building appropriate policies, processes and systems and strictly adhering to the same, as in the case of NALCO.

Talent Management is one of the crucial areas through which HR leverages on the human capital and in the chapter "HR'S Strategic Interventions: A Study Against Miles and Snow Typology", the case depicts how through the specific interventions of Development programme for Middle Managers titled Creating Organisational Performance Excellence (COPE) and Reward and Recognition scheme, HR has truly supported the organisation's strategy. According to Ghoshal (2003, p. 109), the basic proposition in Organisational Strategy Structure and Process (OSSP) is that "successful companies need to develop consistency among their strategy, the business model they adopt, including the choice of technology, and their organisational capability, including human resource practices". The HR strategy adopted in L&T (E&A) typically reflects a strategy suitable to a prospector organisation. Prospectors generally have very elaborate internal communication mechanism and the same is true for L&T E&A, as depicted in Appendix 7. Prospectors put a great emphasis on organisational capability which is nothing but the summation of the competencies of the employees in the organisation. The twin interventions studied depict the great emphasis the organisation puts on behavioural competencies and the mechanism required for reinforcing such competencies.

The singular important change factor today is digitalisation (Mishra, Shukla, & Sujatha., 2017). In the case of "Critical Success Factors in ERP-SAP Implementation and HR", the case shows how HR as Change agent brings about the required change in the company by building systems to focus on the CSFs through the stages of SAP implementation.

Out of all the factors of Production such as land, labour and capital, it is only the human capital which is the most under-utilised. It is said that only 10% of the potential of the brain of executives is successfully tapped by the organisations. It is only the human capital which has unlimited potential to be enhanced through appropriate investments. Further, as the world changes through continuous volatility, human capital is considered as the new foundation of wealth and the source of competitive advantage. The case studies specifically highlighting the various dimensions of changes in organisational as well as HR strategies focus some of the momentous themes highly relevant in today's business world.

The qualitative studies do bring out one dimension clearly that the perceptions of HR and non-HR functions to the same organisational issues are different. This has specifically been examined in the context of OPGC, wherein the views of important stakeholders regarding the relevance of CSFs in each phase of implementation of SAP has been ascertained, examined, compared, both with respect to within OPGC functions as well as vis-à-vis Accenture and also with respect to Esteves and Pastor-Collado (2000) model.

Conclusions, Limitations and Future Research

The analysis of the cases brings out significant correlations between organisational changes and HR's role in strategic or transformational nuances, execution of strategy, organisational restructuring analysis, sustaining organisational change processes, developing or analysing metrics for deliverables for implementing organisational change and so on. The limitation of this study stems from the broadness of the study. No two cases use the same set of variables manifest as HRM practices in the six cases embodied in this book. All six cases take up six distinct dimensions. Hence, comparison of the six companies against a common set of variables, cannot be carried out, which, if conducted, could have led the research to an understanding of possible direct causal relationships between the variables.

The qualitative studies did bring out one dimension clearly that the perceptions of HR and non-HR functions to the same organisational issues are different. This was specifically examined in the context of OPGC, wherein the views of important stakeholders regarding the relevance of CSFs in each phase of implementation of SAP was ascertained, examined and compared, both with respect to within OPGC functions as well as vis-à-vis Accenture and also with respect to Esteves and Pastor-Collado (2000) model and analysis of reasonings as to the variations in perceptions was ascertained, as detailed in Appendix 8.

The qualitative analysis is required to be corroborated through rock-solid data gathered through questionnaire method. The multidimensionality, broadness, level and depth of the objectives of the study against the background of the complexities and volatility of the politico-social, economic, technological and legal environment lead the authors to adopt triangulation methodology for completing the study. As the authors take their study to the next level, the results of the quantitative research shall be brought about by the authors in a different book.

Appendices

Appendix 1

List of Companies with Period and Nature of Organisational Changes

Table A1 List of Companies With Period and Nature of Organisational Changes

Sl. No.	Organisation	Company Type	Sector/Industry	Type of organisational change	Period of Change
1	Aditya Birla Group	Private	Diversified	Merger & Acquisition	Ongoing
2	Air India	Public	Airline	Merger & Acquisition	2007 – Onwards
3	Asian Paints	Private	Paint	Technological interventions	2000 Onwards
4	Blue Dart	MNC	Courier & Package Distribution	Merger & Acquisition	2005 Onwards
5	BNP PARIBAS	MNC	Financial Services	Technological Interventions	Ongoing
6	Cadbury	MNC	Confectionery	Merger & Acquisition	2010-onwards
7	Computer Maintenance Corporation	Private	IT	Merger & Acquisition	2001–2015
8	eBay Inc	MNC	e-Commerce	Technological Interventions	2008 Onwards
9	Etihad Airways	MNC	Airline	Merger & Acquisition	2013 Onwards
10	GE	MNC	Diversified	Business Expansion	Ongoing
11	General Motor	MNC	Automotive	Growth	2010–2011
12	HCL Technologies	Private	IT	Growth	2005 Onwards
13	Infosys	Private	IT	Growth	2003–2006

(Continued)

Table A1 (Continued)

Sl. No.	Organisation	Company Type	Sector/Industry	Type of organisational change	Period of Change
14	Jaguar Land Rover	MNC	Automotive	Merger & Acquisition	2008 Onwards
15	JSPL	Private	Steel & Power	Business Expansion	2007- Onwards
16	L&T (E&A)	Private	Electrical & Automation	Business Expansion	2013- Onwards
17	Mahindra & Mahindra	Private	Automotive & Farm Equipment	Business Expansion	Two major Phases: one in 1993 another in 2010
18	Motorola	MNC	Telecommunications	Business Expansion	2004–2006
19	NALCO	Public	Aluminium	Business Expansion	1981 Onwards
20	NTPC Limited	Public	Power	Growth	2002–2007
21	Nicholas Piramal Group	Private	Diversified	Merger & Acquisition	1997–1998
22	NTPC-SAIL Power Company Private Limited (NSPCL)	Public	Power	Merger & Acquisition	2001 – Contd.
23	Odisha Power Generation Corporation Ltd. (OPGC)	Public Private Partnership	Power	Merger & Acquisition	Ongoing
24	Oil & Natural Gas Corporation Limited (ONGC)	Public	Oil	Business Expansion	Ongoing
25	Paradeep Phosphates Limited (PPL)	MNC	fertiliser	Merger & Acquisition	2002–Contd.

26	RITES	Public	Engineering Consultancy	Business Expansion	Ongoing
27	Syntheite	Private	manufacturer of value-added Spices, Oleoresins and Essential Oils	Business Expansion	2008–Ongoing
28	Tata Consultancy Services (TCS)	Private	IT	Growth	2002 Onwards
29	TATA MOTORS	Private	Automotive	Growth	2001
30	The Raymond Group	Private	Producer and Retailer of Branded Fabric	Business Expansion	2008–Contd.

(Aditya Birla Group, 2020; Air India, 2020; Asian Paints, 2020; Blue Dart, 2021; BNP PARIBAS, 2020; Cadbury, 2020; Computer Maintenance Corporation, 2020; eBay Inc, 2020; Etihad Airways, 2020; GE, 2020; General Motors, 2020; HCL Technologies, 2020; Infosys, 2020; Jaguar Land Rover, 2020; Jindal Steel & Power, 2019; L&T(E&A), 2019; Mahindra & Mahindra, 2020; Motorola, 2020; NALCO, 2020; NTPC, 2021; Nicholas Piramal Group, 2020; NSPCL, 2020; OPGC, 2019; ONGC, 2020; PPL, 2020; RITES, 2020; Syntheite, 2020; TCS, 2020; TATA MOTORS, 2020; The Raymond Group, 2020)

Appendix 2

Collation of Number of Interviewees

Table A2 Collation of Number of Interviewees

Designation/Levels	Blue Dart	JSPL	NTPC	NALCO	L&T (E&A)	OPGC	Total
CEOs	1	1	1	1	1	1	6
HOHRs	1	1	1	1	1		5
CFOs/HoFinance	1	1	1	1	1	1	6
Departmental Heads (Line)	4	6	8	4	3	9	34
Middle Level Executives	5	6	5	5	4	12	37
Working Level Employees				11		3	14
Union/Association Leaders		3	5	16			24
Total	12	18	21	39	10	26	126

Appendix 3
Schedule of Interviews

1. Could you please briefly touch upon the evolution of your organisation in terms of business along with Major milestones. (This may include Organisational profiling – Business, Financial numbers (maybe over last 10 years), Structure, people, processes, initial challenges in creation of the company, organisational growth over the years with timeline.)

2. How have the change in business and strategy at corporate, business and operational levels occurred at the competitive landscape over the years? Could you please elaborate on a few changes?

3. What is the role of HR department and HR function in organisational change? Could you elaborate such role in Pre-implementation, during implementation and after implementation stages?

4. What have been the HR systems developed – target deliverables and HR metrics? What are the HR programmes, policies, practices and processes developed and strategically designed for change to happen?

5. What has been the level of Integration between Organisational structure and HR strategy, and also between the organisational and HR structure before and after the change?

6. Were specific competencies identified or developed to bring the change? What have been the CSFs?

7. What has been the impact of change on the growth or stability of the organisation (revenue, customer base, growth per employee, etc.)?

8. What have been the challenges faced in leveraging the process of change?

9. (In case of MNC) What do you consider the country of origin effect in your organisation? How do you reconcile the conflicting forces for global efficiencies and national differentiation or effecting "global localisation"?

(N.B.: The identity of the interviewees would be kept confidential)

Appendix 4

Financials of the Case Companies

Blue Dart Financials

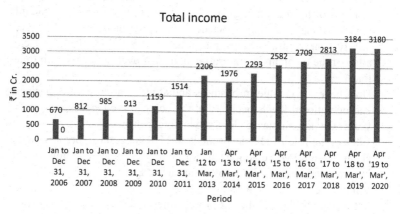

Figure A4.1 Blue Dart: Total Annual Income

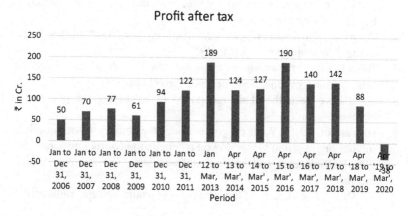

Figure A4.2 Blue Dart: Profit after Tax

NTPC Financials

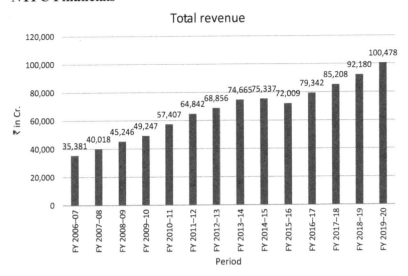

Figure A4.3 NTPC: Total Revenue

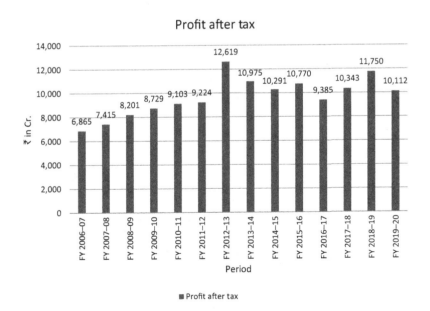

Figure A4.4 NTPC: Profit After Tax

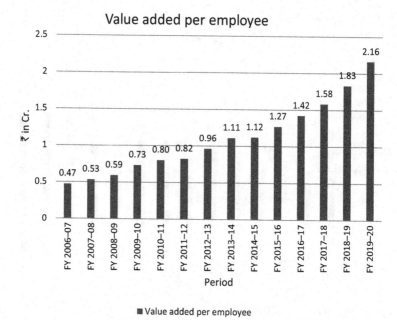

Figure A4.5 NTPC: Value Added per Employee

JSPL's Financial Position

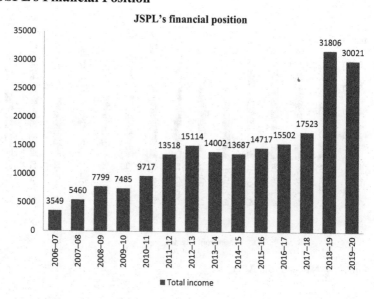

Figure A4.6 JSPL: Total Income

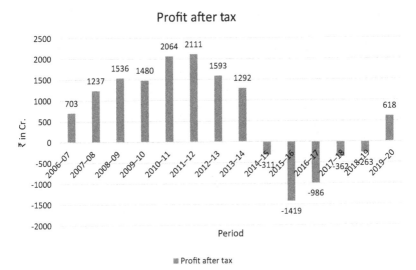

Figure A4.7 JSPL: Profit After Tax

NALCO's Financial Position

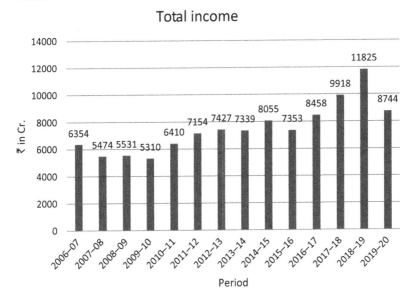

Figure A4.8 NALCO: Total Income

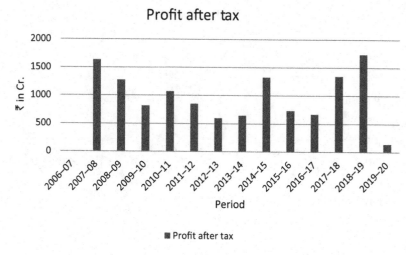

Figure A4.9 NALCO: Profit After Tax

Financial Position of L&T (E&A)

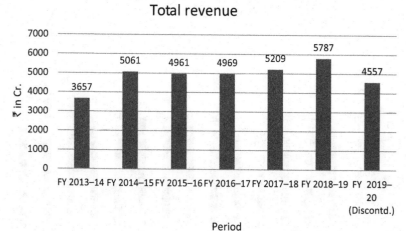

Figure A4.10 Financials: L&T (Electrical & Automation)

OPGC – Financial Position

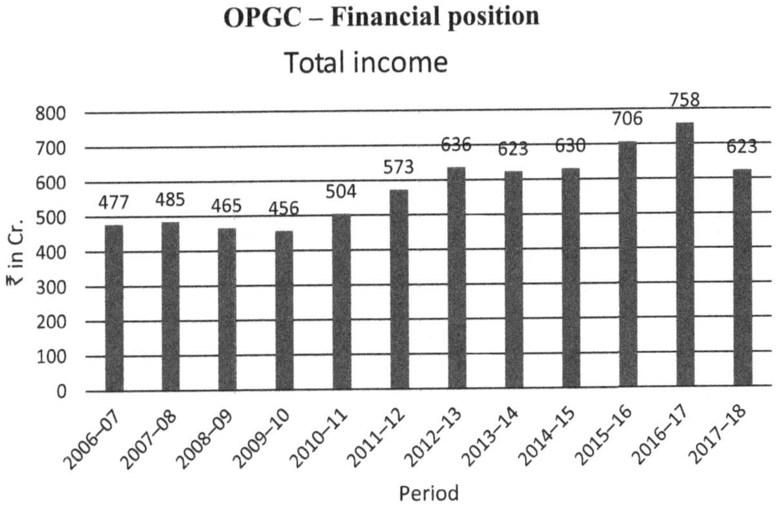

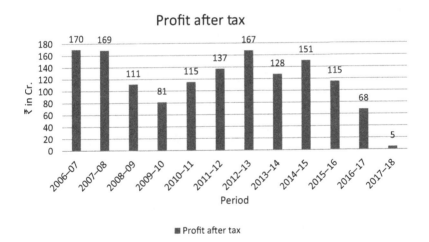

Figure A4.11 OPGC: Total Income

Figure A4.12 OPGC: Profit After Tax

Appendix 5
List of Unions in NALCO

Table A5 List of Unions in NALCO

Sl. No.	Name of the Union	Regn. & Date	Year of Regn.	Affiliation & No.	Function Unit/Office	Remarks
01	Nalco Shramik Congress Union	1443 19.11.1982	1982	INTUC 8661/88	CPP, Nalco Nagar, Dist: Angul (Orissa)- **Recognised**	Captive Power Plant
02	Nalco Non-Executive Employees Union	1687 06.05.1986	1986	HMS	CPP, Nalco Nagar, Dist: Angul (Orissa)	
03	Nalco Vidyut Mazdoor Sangh	SBP-26 10.08.1990	1990	BMS	CPP, Nalco Nagar, Dist: Angul (Orissa)	
04	Nalco Industrial Workers Union	SBP-29/90	1990	CITU	CPP, Nalco Nagar, Dist: Angul (Orissa)	
05	Nalco Bidyut Shramik Sangha	–	2003	–	CPP, Nalco Nagar, Dist: Angul (Orissa)	
06	Nalco Karmachari Sangh	1515 12.10.1983	1983	INTUC 7669	Smelter, Nalco Nagar, Dist: Angul (Orissa)	Smelter
07	Nalco Progressive Employees' Union	1497 30.07.1983	1983	HMS	Smelter, Nalco Nagar, Dist: Angul (Orissa)	
08	Aluminium Mazdoor Sangh	1794	1987	BMS 0/14	Smelter, Nalco Nagar, Dist: Angul (Orissa)	

No.	Union	Reg. No./Date	Year	Affiliation	Location	Unit
09	Nalco Smelter Workers Union	145/SBP 02.02.1998	1998	AITUC	Smelter, Nalco Nagar, Dist: Angul (Orissa)	
10	Nalco Employees Sangh	197/SBP 29.08.2001	2001	INTUC 11422	Smelter, Nalco Nagar, Dist: Angul (Orissa) – **Recognised**	
11	Nalco Smelter Shramik Sangh	193/SBP 07.08.2001	2001	CITU	Smelter Division, Nalco Nagar, Dist: Angul (Orissa)	Smelter Division
12	Nalco Employees Union	1500 25.08.1983	1983	INTUC 9049 14.08.1989	Alumina Refinery, Damanjodi, Dist: Koraput (Orissa)	Alumina Refinery
13	Nalco Mazdoor Sangh	14	1989	BMS & PSENC 48/92	Alumina Refinery, Damanjodi, Dist: Koraput (Orissa)- **Recognised**	
14	M&R Employees Union	–	1987	CITU	Both Alumina Refinery & Mine Unit, Damanjodi, Dist: Koraput (Orissa)	Both Alumina Refinery & Mine Unit
15	Nalco Employees Association	–	1996	–	Both Alumina Refinery &Mine Unit, Damanjodi, Dist: Koraput (Orissa)	
16	Nalco Mines Employees Union	28/JYP 06.06.1990	1990	INTUC	Mines Unit, Damanjodi, Dist: Koraput (Orissa)- **Recognised**	Mines Unit
17	Nalco Mines Mazdoor Sangh	178	1997	BMS 0/86	Mines Unit, Damanjodi, Dist: Koraput (Orissa)	
18	Nalco LDP Employees Union	265/JYP 28.08.2000	2000	–	Both Alumina Refinery & Mines, Damanjodi, Dist: Koraput (Orissa)	Both Alumina Refinery & Mines
19	Nalco Employees Technical Association	272/JYP	2000	HMS	Both Alumina Refinery & Mines, Damanjodi, Dist: Koraput (Orissa)	Both Alumina Refinery & Mines

(Continued)

Table A5 (Continued)

Sl. No.	Name of the Union	Regn. & Date	Year of Regn.	Affiliation & No.	Function Unit/Office	Remarks
20	Nalco Employees Central Union	1490/83 06.07.1993	1983	BMS	Corporate Office, P/1, Nayapalli, Bhubaneswar	Corporate Office, P/1, Nayapalli, Bhubaneswar
21	Nalco Employees Association	444/94	1994	CITU OR-108	Corporate Office, P/1, Nayapalli, Bhubaneswar	
22	Nalco Corporate Employees Union	590-CTC 13.08.1997	1997	–	Corporate Office, P/1, Nayapalli, Bhubaneswar	
23	Nalco Shramik Sangh	704-CTC	2000	BMS	Corporate Office, P/1, Nayapalli, Bhubaneswar	
24	Nalco Employees Forum	816/CTC	2004	–	Corporate Office, P/1, Nayapalli, Bhubaneswar	
25	Nalco Employees Association	–	1983	–	New Delhi Office, New Delhi	New Delhi Office
26	Nalco Employees Association	1891/84	1984	–	Kolkata Office, Kolkata	Kolkata Office
27	Nalco Mines Operators Union	338/JYP 22.09.2004	2004	–	Panchapatmali Bauxite Mines, Damanjodi	Panchapatmali Bauxite Mines
28	Alumina Refinery Progressive Union	–	2004	–	Refinery, Damanjodi	Refinery
29	Nalco Employees Union (P.F.)	D/2062/2008	2008	–	Port Facilities, Vizag	Port Facilities

Appendix 6

Salient Points of Unit-Level and Organisation-Level Awards at L&T (E&A)

Table A6.1 L&T (E&A) Unit Level Awards

Award Name	Frequency	Key Points
e-Appreciation Award (Team)	As & When required (Team)	• Any significant efforts done by the team could be recognised by superiors immediately.
STAR TEAM Award	Quarterly (Team)	• Significant achievement by a team • Financial/Customer/Processes • Reward Points worth Rs 2,000, Award Certificates
QUANTUM LEAP PROJECT Award	Quarterly (Team)	• Best Improvement Projects-Line Managers • Quality/Cost Reduction/Delivery time • Reward Points worth up to Rs 5,000 for each member
GROUND-BREAKER INNOVATION Award	Quarterly (Common-Individual/Team)	• Best Innovations successfully implemented at each Unit Level • Benefits/Freshness/ Reward Points worth Rs 10,000 (Individual) or Rs 5,000 per member (Team)
HUMANITARIAN CHAMPION Award	Annually (Common-Individual/Team)	• Demonstrate Spirit of Humanity • Volunteer work/CSR Projects/ Supports colleagues • Reward Points worth Rs 10K (Individual) or Rs 5,000 per member (Team)

Table A6.2 Organisation Level Awards – Team

Award Name	Frequency	Key Points
ACE TEAM Award	Annually (Team)	Significant Achievement by a TEAM having an organisation-wide impact Balanced Scorecard approach Reward points worth Rs 5,000 Golden Shield
ACE Project Award	Annually (Team)	Best Improvement project by a team having an organisation-wide impact Reward points worth Rs 10,000, Golden Shield
HE Excellence Award	Annually (Team)	Recognise the best HR team across SBUs and respective locations Reward points worth Rs 2,000 per member, Golden Shield, Annual HR meet

Table A6.3 L&T (E&A) Organisation Level Awards: Common – Individual/Team

Award Name	Frequency	Key Points
ACE INNOVATION Award	As &When required (Common-Individual/Team)	• Best Innovations successfully implemented at organisational level • Benefits, Freshness, Reward Points worth Rs 20,000 or Rs 10,000 per member (Team)
ACE INTELLECT Award	As &When required (Common-Individual/Team)	• Reward Patents & Designs which generate exceptional value for organisation • Cash rewards of Rs. 12,000, Rs. 2,500 for patents & Designs, respectively, at time filing as well as granted
ACE PUBLICATION Award	As &When required (Common-Individual/Team)	• Reward Articles/Paper published in journals/ newspapers or conferences • Cash rewards as high as Rs. 7,000 FOR international journals/conferences

Appendix 7

Communication Mechanism in L&T (E&A)

Table A7 Communication Mechanism in L&T (E&A)

Forum	Objective	Periodicity
PACE workshops	Annual Objective setting workshops where Seniors communicate Org Strategy, SBU/Dept goals	Annual
Town Hall meetings	All employees connect with the Leadership – sharing updates and hearing the employee voice	As and when Leaders visit sites
HR Connect	HR Leadership communication with Site employees. HR practises, Employee benefits, new initiatives, etc. and addressing employee issues/concerns	Quarterly
Code of Conduct/Ethics	To develop awareness and adherence to CoC and Corp Governance issues	All employees covered once a year
Union meetings with Seniors	Understanding issues and concerns and communicating top management views and plans	Quarterly
Internal Web Portal	Discussion forums, blogs, news, updates	Regularly
E&A HR News	Mailers communicating, Business-related issues, achievements, future plans, new hires, superannuation, changes in policies, etc.	As and when
Induction program	For new hires where Senior Leaders and HR Leaders address employees	Once in 2 months
Display boards in offices/factory	Time to time communication. Best practises, HR initiatives and other updates	
Elite meetings	Sharing Best innovative practises within company and address by Senior Leadership	Annual

Appendix 8
CSF Relevance along the ASAP Implementation Phases

Table A8 Relevance of CSFs Along Phases of SAP Implementation

CSF Relevance along the ASAP Implementation Phases		Phase I (Project Preparation)						
		Esteves & Pastor-Collado (2000) Theoretical Model	Internal Rating (OPGC)	External Rating (Accenture)	Rating of HR	Rating of TLs (Technical)	Overall Rating	Analysis
Organisational Perspective	Sustained Management Support	High	High	Normal	High	High	High	The work during the first phase revolves around finalisation of work plan, budget analysis, etc. These are mostly internal jobs. Hence, the differential perception.
	Effective Organisational Change	Low	Normal	Low	High	Normal	Normal	Internal change management is mostly the responsibility of HR and top Management.
	Good Project Scope Management	Normal	Normal	Normal	High	Normal	Normal	HR is the most complex module in the SAP, as HR practices differ from organisation to organisation. Hence, the variation.

Adequate Project Team Composition	Normal	**High**	**High**	Normal	**High**	**High**	The success of the implementation is always based on the way the stipulations are spelt out in the project. An adequate Project Team can only ensure this. Hence, high relevance.
Meaningful Business Process Reengineering	Normal	Normal	Normal	Normal	Normal	Normal	There is no discrepancy vis-à-vis Model. Further, all segments feel that it is of normal relevance.
User involvement and participation	Normal	**High**	Normal	**High**	**High**	Normal	The views of internal stakeholders stem from the complexities of the organisation.
Project Champion Role	**High**	**High**	Normal	**High**	**High**	Normal	External Consultants may feel that a company which is implementing SAP would already be having a Project Champion. In case of OPGC, it did not have the requisite competency in any internal resources and had to hire a person who would work as a project champion to implement the project; hence this difference in perception.

(Continued)

Table A8 (Continued)

CSF Relevance along the ASAP Implementation Phases	Phase I (Project Preparation)						Analysis
	Esteves & Pastor-Collado (2000) Theoretical Model	Internal Rating (OPGC)	External Rating (Accenture)	Rating of HR	Rating of TLs (Technical)	Overall Rating	
Trust between Partners	Normal	High	High	High	High	High	OPGC Employees were governed under diversified compensation structures and multifarious service conditions – viz. erstwhile employees from Government cadre, new Market-Based Salary cadre, Project roll, direct contracts, outsourced resources, employees of strategic partner through resource sharing, etc.; hence, in OPGC, trust building was considered to be of high relevance.

Dedicated Staff and Consultants	Normal	High	High	High	High	High	A group of dedicated staff, together with external consultants, can form a close-knit, focused and motivated group that can work without communication problems. Hence, a great emphasis.
Strong Communications Inward and Outwards	Normal	High	High	High	Normal	High	Where communication stops, rumour mongering and grapevines take over. Communication is the primary responsibility of HR, which gets reflected in the importance attached by HR.
Formalised Project Plan/ Schedule	High	High	High	High	Normal	High	Since in this phase, detailed Project plan is created, all segments have rated this CSF high, except some TLs of Technical functions.
Adequate Training Program	Normal	Normal	Normal	High	Low	Normal	HR feels that even at the planning stage, training sessions to create the mental readiness for acceptance of the change may be required.
Preventive Troubleshooting	Normal	Normal	Low	Normal	Normal	Normal	No difference in perception as against the Model.

(*Continued*)

Table A8 (Continued)

CSF Relevance along the ASAP Implementation Phases

	Phase 1 (Project Preparation)							
	Esteves & Pastor-Collado (2000) Theoretical Model	Internal Rating (OPGC)	External Rating (Accenture)	Rating of HR	Rating of TLs (Technical)	Overall Rating	Analysis
Usage of Appropriate Consultant	Normal	Normal	**High**	**High**	**High**	**High**	The phase involves activities such as setting up the initial system landscape based on the technical requirement, planning deliverables, developing system administration procedures, etc. and thus prepares the edifice for the SAP roll-out. This explains why high importance is attached.
Empowered Decision Makers	Low	Normal	**High**	**High**	Normal	**High**	Decision-making about planning and schedules is as important during planning stage as later. HR and Accenture feel that empowerment in decision making would help decide on the processes and facilitate coming up with perfect business blueprint.

Technical Perspectivea							
Adequate ERP Implementation Strategy	Normal	High	High	High	High	High	Important strategies, such as Change Management and Communication Strategy and Plan, Project Management Strategy, Plan and Schedule, etc. are to be carried out at this stage. Hence, the high importance.
Avoid Customisation	Normal	Normal	Normal	High	Low	Normal	Since there are a lot many areas in HR in OPGC, which are not as per the standardised module of SAP and since OPGC was 51% government-owned company, HR felt that migration to SAP may require too much of customisation.
Adequate ERP Version	Normal	Normal	Normal	High	Normal	Normal	EPR version, from HR point of view, is of high importance as the HR approach changes with changing times.

(Continued)

Table A8 (Continued)

CSF Relevance along the ASAP Implementation Phases	Phase I (Project Preparation)						
	Esteves & Pastor-Collado (2000) Theoretical Model	Internal Rating (OPGC)	External Rating (Accenture)	HR Rating	Technical TL Rating	Overall Rating	Analysis
Adequate Software Configuration	Normal	Normal	Low	**High**	Normal	Normal	Traditional modular SAP-HR system includes the functional organisational structure management, personnel administration, time management and payroll accounting. However, quite often, HR process requires additional software configuration, such as for presenting the organisational structure in a graphical formation, etc. The standard tools offered by SAP are inadequate. These explain HR giving importance at this stage.
Adequate Legacy System Knowledge	Low	Normal	**High**	**High**	**High**	**High**	In OPGC, there are a lot of legacy issues and most of the users would like to have the software configured in the same way as legacy system. Hence the importance to legacy system knowledge.

CSF Relevance along the ASAP Implementation Phases		Phase II (Business Blueprinting)						
		Esteves & Pastor-Collado (2000) Theoretical Model	Internal Rating (OPGC)	External Rating (Accenture)	HR Rating	Technical TL Rating	Overall Rating	Analysis
Organisational Perspective	Sustained Management Support	Normal	High	Normal	High	High	High	The business blueprint is a detailed process-oriented and technical documentation of the results based on service description. Internal Team considers this CSF important, so that the "to be" business processes can be finalised in time.
	Effective Organisational Change	High	High	Normal	High	Normal	Normal	Since the stage involves codifying the "to be" process, it requires effective organisational change insight and hence the high rating accorded by some segments.
	Good Project Scope Management	Normal	Normal	High	Normal	Normal	High	Project Scope management is of high importance from vendor's perspective, as it directly impacts the timeline and cost of the Project. Hence, Accenture rates the CSF as highly relevant.

(Continued)

Table A8 (Continued)

CSF Relevance along the ASAP Implementation Phases	Phase II (Business Blueprinting)						
	Esteves & Pastor-Collado (2000) Theoretical Model	Internal Rating (OPGC)	External Rating (Accenture)	HR Rating	Technical TL Rating	Overall Rating	Analysis
Adequate Project Team Composition	Normal	**High**	**High**	**High**	Normal	**High**	HR and Accenture both feel that in blueprinting/design phase, composition of the team plays a vital role, as it drafts and finalises the processes.
Meaningful Business Process Reengineering	Normal	Normal	**High**	Normal	Normal	**Normal**	BPR involves changes in the way of doing business; it is changing the way of working of an organisation and the process-oriented vision that organisation needs to integrate. OPGC is a government company and its processes are open to audit. Employees have a right to go on writ and also seek information under Right to Information Act. Hence, business processes of the organisation are relatively rigid. This explains why the Internal stakeholders attach normal (and not High) relevance to this CSF.

Factor							Comments
User involvement and participation	High	High	Normal	High	High	High	Creating the blueprint involves understanding and illustrating what department or individual is responsible for what part of the process from beginning to end and where and how the handoffs between departments occur.
Project Champion Role	High	High	Normal	High	High	High	Except Accenture, all feel that Project Champion role is of high relevance in Phase II, as the Project champion has to co-ordinate with all Departments for finalising the blueprint.
Trust between Partners	Normal	High	High	High	Normal	High	The analysis is the same as contained in Phase I for the CSF.
Dedicated Staff and Consultants	Normal	High	High	High	Normal	High	The analysis is the same as contained in Phase I for the CSF.

(Continued)

Table A8 (Continued)

CSF Relevance along the ASAP Implementation Phases	Phase II (Business Blueprinting)						
	Esteves & Pastor-Collado (2000) Theoretical Model	Internal Rating (OPGC)	External Rating (Accenture)	HR Rating	Technical TL Rating	Overall Rating	Analysis
Strong Communications Inward and Outwards	Normal	High	High	High	High	High	Steering Committee, Business Sponsorship Group, Process owners and SAP Core Team need to understand and drive the vision/purpose/benefits of SAP Implementation Project, while others need to have general awareness of the SAP Implementation Project and its objectives. Because of the complexities of the organisation, it has been rated high at this stage.
Formalised Project Plan/ Schedule	Normal	Normal	High	High	Normal	High	There is a necessity of strict adherence to the schedule of blue printing, which requires voluminous work, hence rated high by some segments.

Adequate Training Program	Normal	Normal	Normal	**High**	Normal	Normal	Since blueprint stage basically captures the "As is" and "To Be" process, all segments have rated this CSF as "normal". However, HR feels the need of adequate training as it would help documentation.
Preventive Troubleshooting	Normal	Normal	Normal	Normal	Normal	Normal	No discrepancy vis-à-vis the Model.
Usage of Appropriate Consultant	Normal	**High**	**High**	**High**	**High**	**High**	Every stakeholder feels that appropriate functional consultants with relevant experience in the modules and process are required for defining the final "to be" business processes. This concern stems from the complexity of the organisation.
Empowered Decision Makers	Normal	**High**	**High**	**High**	Normal	**High**	Except for technical team, stakeholders feel that the empowerment of decision makers will help formulate the design quickly.

(Continued)

Table A8 (Continued)

CSF Relevance along the ASAP Implementation Phases		Phase II (Business Blueprinting)						
		Esteves & Pastor-Collado (2000) Theoretical Model	Internal Rating (OPGC)	External Rating (Accenture)	HR Rating	Technical TL Rating	Overall Rating	Analysis
Technical Perspective	**Adequate ERP Implementation Strategy**	Normal	High	High	High	High	High	Formulating the "To Be" process requires strategic decision making regarding doing away with ineffective and inefficient processes and embracing new processes already tested in the standard SAP module.
	Avoid Customisation	Normal	Normal	High	High	Low	Normal	Analysis is same as given in Phase I.
	Adequate ERP Version	Normal	Normal	Normal	High	Normal	Normal	The stage mostly involves documentation, hence considered of "normal importance".
	Adequate Software Configuration	Normal	Normal	Normal	High	Normal	Normal	Regarding the rating of HR, analysis is same as given in Phase I.

	Esteves & Pastor-Collado (2000) Theoretical Model	Internal Rating (OPGC)	External Rating (Accenture)	HR Rating	Technical TL Rating	Overall Rating	Analysis
Adequate Legacy System Knowledge	Normal	High	High	High	High	High	During the blueprinting, employees use the knowledge of legacy system for the business process definition, map it to the new system and finally prepare the new business process document. This explains the rating.

CSF Relevance along the ASAP Implementation Phases

Phase III (Business Realisation)

	Esteves & Pastor-Collado (2000) Theoretical Model	Internal Rating (OPGC)	External Rating (Accenture)	HR Rating	Technical TL Rating	Overall Rating	Analysis
Organisational Perspective	**Sustained Management Support** — Normal	High	Normal	High	High	High	Sustained Management support would help mobilise the end users for testing and give inputs during building of the system. Hence, the emphasis.
	Effective Organisational Change — Normal	Normal	Normal	High	Normal	Normal	Since bringing about change is essentially a function of HR, the CSF has been rated as "High" by HR.

(Continued)

Table A8 (Continued)

CSF Relevance along the ASAP Implementation Phases	Phase III (Business Realisation)						
	Esteves & Pastor-Collado (2000) Theoretical Model	Internal Rating (OPGC)	External Rating (Accenture)	HR Rating	Technical TL Rating	Overall Rating	Analysis
Good Project Scope Management	Normal	Normal	**High**	Normal	Normal	**High**	Analysis is same as for Phase II.
Adequate Project Team Composition	Normal	Normal	Normal	**High**	Normal	Normal	A good team can rigorously test the system and make the system better and error-free, building adequate team is a deliverable of HR.
Meaningful Business Process Reengineering	Normal	Normal	**High**	Normal	Normal	Normal	Analysis is same as for Phase II.
User involvement and participation	**High**	**High**	**High**	**High**	Normal	**High**	Most of the processes in technical areas conform to the standardised SAP processes. Hence, a differential perception.

Project Champion Role	High	High	Normal	High	High	Normal	Accenture considers this of normal relevance, as Champion's involvement in this "build stage" is less. However, others feel the role is crucial in each stage.
Trust between Partners	Normal	Normal	High	High	Normal	High	The analysis is same as contained in Phase I & II.
Dedicated Staff and Consultants	Normal	Normal	High	High	Normal	High	Many stakeholders have attached importance for proper and timely building of the system.
Strong Communications Inward and Outwards	Normal	Normal	High	High	Normal	High	Because of complexities of the organisation, it has got overall rating "high" at this stage.
Formalised Project Plan/ Schedule	Normal	Normal	High	High	Normal	Normal	The overall rating has been normal which is in synch with the theoretical model.
Adequate Training Program	Normal	Normal	High	Normal	High	Normal	Some segments have given high importance, as the end-users should be made aware of the extent of the impact of the solution at this stage.
Preventive Troubleshooting	Normal	Normal	High	Normal	Normal	Normal	From Accenture's point of view, they need to be ready for the next phase when the actual testing takes place.

(Continued)

Table A8 (Continued)

CSF Relevance along the ASAP Implementation Phases		Phase III (Business Realisation)						
		Esteves & Pastor-Collado (2000) Theoretical Model	Internal Rating (OPGC)	External Rating (Accenture)	HR Rating	Technical TL Rating	Overall Rating	Analysis
	Usage of Appropriate Consultant	Normal	**High**	**High**	**High**	**High**	**High**	The analysis as given at Phase II is also true for the build and test phase.
	Empowered Decision Makers	Normal	Normal	**High**	**High**	Normal	**High**	The reason for high rating by these segments is because empowered decision-making can help facilitate the test approach plan. Hence, emphasis by Accenture and HR.
Technical Perspective	**Adequate ERP Implementation Strategy**	Normal	Normal	**High**	**High**	Normal	Normal	The reason for high rating by Accenture and HR is because adequate ERP Implementation strategy can help facilitate the test approach plan.
	Avoid Customisation	Normal	Normal	**High**	**High**	**Low**	Normal	The analysis given at Phase I for this CSF also explains discrepancy vis-à-vis Model in ratings of HR & Accenture.

	Esteves & Pastor-Collado (2000) Theoretical Model	Internal Rating (OPGC)	External Rating (Accenture)	HR Rating	Technical TL Rating	Overall Rating	Analysis
Adequate ERP Version	Normal	Normal	**High**	**High**	Normal	Normal	External agency has rated it as of "High relevance", considering the fact that during build phase, proper version and updates of the ERP must be ensured while installing the application.
Adequate Software Configuration	**High**	**High**	**High**	**High**	**High**	**High**	No discrepancy vis-à-vis Model.
Adequate Legacy System Knowledge	Normal	Normal	Normal	**High**	Normal	Normal	To complete the testing one has to have sound knowledge of all processes and hence HR has rated this CSF as of high relevance.

CSF Relevance along the ASAP Implementation Phases

Phase IV (Final Preparation)

	Esteves & Pastor-Collado (2000) Theoretical Model	Internal Rating (OPGC)	External Rating (Accenture)	HR Rating	Technical TL Rating	Overall Rating	Analysis
Organisational Perspective **Sustained Management Support**	Normal	Normal	Normal	Normal	**High**	Normal	Not much of discrepancy vis-à-vis Model, except for the ratings of technical TLs.

(Continued)

Table A8 (Continued)

CSF Relevance along the ASAP Implementation Phases	Phase IV (Final Preparation)						
	Esteves & Pastor-Collado (2000) Theoretical Model	Internal Rating (OPGC)	External Rating (Accenture)	HR Rating	Technical TL Rating	Overall Rating	Analysis
Effective Organisational Change	Normal	Normal	Normal	**High**	Normal	Normal	HR rates this CSF high at this stage. This is because sharing of data by the user is important for uploading the same in the system and sometimes employees feel insecure parting with the data as the organisational change takes place.
Good Project Scope Management	Normal	Normal	Normal	**High**	Normal	Normal	Analysis is same as for Phase I.
Adequate Project Team Composition	Normal	Normal	Normal	**High**	Normal	Normal	Employees play an important role in the final preparation for cut-over stage, which requires best team effort for ensuring that the correct/updated master data is uploaded in the system for testing. Hence, the emphasis by HR.

Meaningful Business Process Reengineering	Normal	Normal	Normal	High	Normal	Normal	In OPGC, most of the changes in processes due to BPR, relate to HR. The actual ramifications of changes become visible to HR from Phase IV onwards, which explains such rating at this stage.
User involvement and participation	Normal	Normal	High	High	High	Normal	Accenture and HR feel that the CSF is of high relevance, as most of the changes in processes relate to HR and the final testing is to be carried out by the users only.
Project Champion Role	High	High	Normal	High	High	High	Not much of discrepancy vis-à-vis Model.
Trust between Partners	Normal	Normal	High	High	Normal	High	The analysis is same as contained in Phase I & II for the CSF.
Dedicated Staff and Consultants	Normal	Normal	High	High	Normal	High	For the success of the Project, the CSF is of high relevance for HR and Accenture.
Strong Communications Inward and Outwards	Normal	Normal	High	High	Normal	High	Proper understanding of the changes requires incessant communication. This explains an overall "high" rating.

(Continued)

Table A8 (Continued)

CSF Relevance along the ASAP Implementation Phases	Phase IV (Final Preparation)						
	Esteves & Pastor-Collado (2000) Theoretical Model	Internal Rating (OPGC)	External Rating (Accenture)	HR Rating	Technical TL Rating	Overall Rating	Analysis
Formalised Project Plan/Schedule	Normal	Normal	High	High	Normal	Normal	Same Analysis as in previous phases.
Adequate Training Program	Normal	High	High	High	High	High	All stakeholders consider that adequate training is required during this stage so that everyone gets ready for using the system after "go live".
Preventive Troubleshooting	High	High	High	High	Normal	High	Tracking and fixing problems before SAP implementation goes into production phase can save a lot of time and money. Hence, high importance.
Usage of Appropriate Consultant	Normal	High	High	High	Normal	High	Stakeholders consider that appropriate consultants are required during the development phase as this is the most crucial phase to prepare the system for going live.
Empowered Decision Makers	Normal	Normal	High	High	Normal	Normal	

Technical Perspective	Normal	Normal	**High**	Normal	
Adequate ERP Implementation Strategy	Normal	Normal	**High**	Normal	Not much discrepancy vis-à-vis Model.
Avoid Customisation	Normal	**High**	**High**	Normal	Avoiding customisation saves time, effort and money, apart from standardising the process as per the SAP best practices and hence high relevance by Accenture and HR.
Adequate ERP Version	Normal	Normal	**High**	Normal	No discrepancy vis-à-vis Model in overall rating.
Adequate Software Configuration	Normal	**High**	**High**	Normal	Both Accenture and HR feel that adequate software configuration is of high relevance.
Adequate Legacy System Knowledge	Normal	Normal	**High**	Normal	HR being saddled with legal issues, takes this as of high importance.

(Continued)

Table A8 (Continued)

CSF Relevance along the ASAP Implementation Phases		Phase V (Go Live & Support)						
		Esteves & Pastor-Collado (2000) Theoretical Model	Internal Rating (OPGC)	External Rating (Accenture)	HR Rating	Technical TL Rating	Overall Rating	Analysis
Organisational Perspective	**Sustained Management Support**	**High**	**High**	**High**	**High**	Normal	**High**	No discrepancy vis-à-vis Model.
	Effective Organisational Change	Normal	Normal	**High**	**High**	Normal	Normal	This is the cut-over phase when employees are expected to move from working on the existing systems to SAP; hence, effective organisational change is considered as a "highly relevant" CSF by HR and Accenture at this stage.
	Good Project Scope Management	Normal	Normal	Normal	**High**	Normal	Normal	Analysis is same as for Phase I.
	Adequate Project Team Composition	Normal	Normal	Normal	**High**	Normal	Normal	Not much discrepancy vis-à-vis Model.

							Analysis
Meaningful Business Process Reengineering	Normal	Normal	Normal	High	Normal	Normal	Analysis is same as for Phase IV.
User involvement and participation	Normal	High	High	High	High	High	All consider user involvement and participation during go live and post go live is highly required for the successful implementation.
Project Champion Role	High	High	High	High	High	High	No discrepancy vis-à-vis Model at all.
Trust between Partners	Normal	Normal	High	High	Normal	Normal	Accenture and HR rate it as High, as trust between partners is required during post go live for avoiding any conflict, which could eventually be an excuse for non-usage of the system.
Dedicated Staff and Consultants	Normal	Normal	High	High	Normal	High	Accenture and HR emphasise it, as dedicated staff and consultants are required post go live for hand-holding of the users and for resolving discordant issues in effective manner.
Strong Communications Inward and Outwards	High	High	High	High	High	High	Not much discrepancy vis-à-vis model.

(Continued)

Table A8 (Continued)

CSF Relevance along the ASAP Implementation Phases	Phase V (Go Live & Support)						Analysis
	Esteves & Pastor-Collado (2000) Theoretical Model	Internal Rating (OPGC)	External Rating (Accenture)	HR Rating	Technical TL Rating	Overall Rating	
Formalised Project Plan/ Schedule	Normal	Normal	**High**	**High**	Normal	Normal	Overall rating conforms to the Model as "Normal", as most of the Plan and schedule is already formalised.
Adequate Training Program	Normal	Normal	**High**	**High**	Normal	Normal	Mostly stakeholders feel that training programmes should be completed before this stage.
Preventive Troubleshooting	Normal	Normal	**Normal**	Normal	Normal	Normal	Not much discrepancy vis-à-vis model.
Usage of Appropriate Consultant	Normal	Normal	**High**	**High**	Normal	Normal	Accenture and HR rate the CSF as "High". Analysis as given in previous phase.
Empowered Decision Makers	Normal	Normal	**Normal**	**Normal**	Normal	Normal	No discrepancy vis-à-vis model.

Technical Perspective						
Adequate ERP Implementation Strategy	Normal	Normal	**Normal**	**Normal**	Normal	No discrepancy vis-à-vis model.
Avoid Customisation	Normal	Normal	**High**	Normal	Normal	Not much discrepancy vis-à-vis model
Adequate ERP Version	Normal	Normal	**Normal**	**Low**	Normal	Not much discrepancy vis-à-vis model.
Adequate Software Configuration	Normal	Normal	**Normal**	Normal	Normal	No discrepancy vis-à-vis model.
Adequate Legacy System Knowledge	Normal	Normal	**High**	Normal	Normal	Analysis as given in previous phase.

References

Adani to acquire. (2020). Retrieved from www.vccircle.com/adani-to-acquire-stake-in-odisha-power-as-aes-exits-after-two-decades/ on 09.03.2021

Aditya Birla Group (2020). Extracted from http://www.adityabirla.com/home on 20.04.2020

Agency Problem. (2019). *Investopedia*. Retrieved from www.investopedia.com/terms/a/agencyproblem.asp on 07.05.2019.

Ahmed, S., & Uddin, S. (2018). Toward a political economy of corporate governance change and stability in family business groups. *Accounting, Auditing & Accountability Journal, 31*(8), 2192–2217.

Ahn, P. S. (2010). *Growth and Decline of Political Unionism in India; Need for a Paradigm Shift* (pp. 11–19). Bangkok: ILO.

Air India (2020). Extracted from https://www.airindia.in/ on 20.04.2020

Ajzen, I., & Fishbein, M. (1980). *Understanding Attitudes and Predicting Social Behaviour*. Englewood Cliffs, NJ: Prentice Hall.

Akbar, M. (2008). Do the governance, strategic and organisational practices differ in Indian family and professionally managed firms? *Vision, 12*(3), 15–30.

Aladwani, A. M. (2001). Change management strategies for successful ERP implementation. *Business Process Management Journal, 7*(3), 266–275.

Ali, A., Chen, T. Y., & Radhakrishnan, S. (2007). Corporate disclosures by family firms. *Journal of Accounting and Economics, 44*(1–2), 238–286.

Al-Mashari, M. (2003). A process change-oriented model for ERP application. *International Journal of Human-Computer Interaction, 16*(1), 39–55.

Altimetrik, Great Place to Work. (2020). Retrieved from www.greatplacetowork.in/great/profile/india-best/Altimetrik-India on 02.02.2021.

Ang, J. S., Cole, R. A., & Lin, J. W. (2000). Agency costs and ownership structure. *The Journal of Finance, 55*(1), 81–106.

Anthony, R. N., Dearden, J., & Vancil, R. F. (1972). *Management Control Systems*. Homewood, IL: R. D. Irwin.

Anwar, S., & Mohsin, R. (2011, January). ERP project management in public sector-key issues and strategies. In *2011 44th Hawaii International Conference on System Sciences* (pp. 1–10). IEEE.

Arnold, J. H. (2000). *History a Very Short Introduction*. Oxford: Oxford University Press.

Aronoff, C. E. (1998). Megatrends in family business. *Family Business Review, 9*(3), 181–185.

Asian Paints (2020). Extracted from https://www.asianpaints.com/ on 20.04.2020

Astrachan, J. (2001). Critical self-review will mature research. In *Family Business Network Newsletter Special Conference Edition* (Vol. 28, pp. 22–24).

Astrachan, J. H., Zahra, S. A., & Sharma, P. (2003). Family-sponsored ventures. Presented in New York on April 29. In *2003 at the First Annual Global Entrepreneurship Symposium: The Entrepreneurial Advantage of Nations*. Retrieved from www.emkf.org/pdf/UN_family_sponsored_report.pdf.

Badri, A., Boudreau-Trudel, B., & Souissi, A. S. (2018). Occupational health and safety in the industry 4.0 era: A cause for major concern? *Safety Science, 109*, 403–411.

Bajaj Finance, Great Place to Work. (2020). Retrieved from www.greatplacetowork. in/great/profile/india-best/Bajaj-Finance on 03.02.2021.

Ballas, A., & Demirakos, E. (2018). The valuation implications of strategy in R&D-intensive industries. *Journal of Applied Accounting Research, 19*(3), 365–382.

Bancroft, N. H., Seip, H., & Sprengel, A. (1998). *Implementing SAP R/3: How to Introduce a Large System into a Large Organization*. Greenwich, CT: Manning Publications.

Bär, K., Herbert-Hansen, Z. N. L., & Khalid, W. (2018). Considering Industry 4.0 aspects in the supply chain for an SME. *Production Engineering, 12*(6), 747–758.

Barth, E., Gulbrandsen, T., & Schonea, P. (2005). Family ownership and productivity: The role of owner-management. *Journal of Corporate Finance, 11*(1–2), 107–127.

Bartlett, C.A., & Ghoshal, S. (1988). Organizing for worldwide effectiveness: The transnational solution. *California Management Review, 31*(1), 54–74.

Bartlett, C.A., & Ghoshal, S. (1995). Changing the role of top management: Beyond structure to processes. *Harvard Business Review, 73*(3), 132–142.

Bartlett, C.A., & Ghoshal, S. (2002). *Managing Across Borders: The Transnational Solution*. Boston, MA: Harvard Business Press.

Beechler, S., & Yang, J.Z. (1994). The transfer of Japanese-style management to American subsidiaries: Contingencies, constraints, and competencies. *Journal of International Business Studies, 25*(3), 467–491.

Bell, R., & Pham, T. T. (2020). Modelling the knowledge transfer process between founder and successor in Vietnamese family businesses succession. *Journal of Family Business Management*. https://doi.org/10.1108/JFBM-03-2020-0024.

Benešová, A., & Tupa, J. (2017). Requirements for education and qualification of people in Industry 4.0. *Procedia Manufacturing, 11*, 2195–2202.

Bennebroek Gravenhorst, K. M., Werkman, R. A., & Boonstra, J. J. (1999). The change capacity of organizations: General assessment and exploring nine configurations. *Power Dynamics and Organisational Change, 3*, 29–54.

Berghe, L. A. A., & Carchon, S. (2003). Agency relations within the family business system: An exploratory approach. *Corporate Governance: An International Review, 11*(3), 171–179.

Bharadwaj, A.S., Bharadwaj, S.G., & Konsynski, B.R. (1999). Information technology effects on firm performance as measured by Tobin's q. *Management Science, 45*(7), 1008–1024.

Bird, B., Welsch, H., Astrachan, J. H., & Pistrui, D. (2002). Family business research: The evolution of an academic field. *Family Business Review, 15*(4), 337–350.

Bjorkman, I., & Lu, Y. (2001). Institutionalization and bargaining power explanations of HRM practices in international joint ventures: The case of Chinese–Western joint ventures. *Organization Studies, 22*(3), 491–512.

Blue Dart. (2021). Retrieved from http://bluedart.com/index.html on 07.03.2021.

BMC, Great Place to Work. (2020). Retrieved from www.greatplacetowork.in/great/profile/india-best/BMC-Software-India on 02.02.2021

Bonekamp, L., & Sure, M. (2015). Consequences of Industry 4.0 on human labour and work organisation. *Journal of Business and Media Psychology, 6*(1), 33–40.

BNP PARIBAS (2020). Extracted from https://group.bnpparibas/en/ on 20.04.2020

Bozer, G., Levin, L., & Santora, J. C. (2017). Succession in family business: multi-source perspectives. Journal of Small Business and Enterprise Development.

Brandl, J., & Pohler, D. (2010). The human resource department's role and conditions that affect its development: Explanations from Austrian CEOs. *Human Resource Management, 49*(6), 1025–1046.

Bratton, J. (1999). Human resource management and industrial relations. In J. Bratton &J. Gold (Eds.), *Human Resource Management: Theory and Practice*. London: Macmillan.

Braun, W. H., & Warner, M. (2002). Strategic human resource management in western multinationals in China: The differentiation of practices across different ownership forms. *Personnel Review, 31*(5), 553–579.

Brewster, C., Wood, G., & Brookes, M. (2008). Similarity, isomorphism or duality? Recent survey evidence on the human resource management policies of multinational corporations. *British Journal of Management, 19*, 320–342.

Brunsson, N. (1989). Administrative reforms as routines. *Scandinavian Journal of Management, 5*(3), 219–228.

Brunsson, N., & Olsen, J. P. (1993). *The Reforming Organisation*. London: Routledge.

Budhwar, P., & Varma, A. (2011). Emerging HR management trends in India and the way forward. *Organizational Dynamics, 40*(4), 317–325.

Bullen, C. V., & Rockart, J. F. (1981). *A Primer on Critical Success Factors*. Center for Information Systems Research, Sloan School of Management, Massachusetts Institute of Technology.

Cadbury (2020). Extracted from https://www.cadbury.co.uk/ on 20.04.2020

Cadence, Great Place to Work. (2020). Retrieved from www.greatplacetowork.in/great/profile/india-best/Cadence-Design-Systems on 02.02.2021.

Caralli, R. A., Stevens, J. F., Willke, B. J., & Wilson, W. R. (2004). *The Critical Success Factor Method: Establishing a Foundation for Enterprise Security Management* (No. CMU/SEI-2004-TR-010). Pittsburgh, PA: Carnegie-Mellon University, Software Engineering Institute.

Carney, M. (2005). Corporate governance and competitive advantage in family-controlled firms. *Entrepreneurship Theory and Practice, 29*(3), 249–265.

CEAT, Great Place to Work. (2020). Retrieved from www.greatplacetowork.in/great/profile/india-best/CEAT on 02.02.2021

Cela, A., & Gatto, S. (2018). *Multi-domestic MNCs that Undertake Global Integration: HRM Convergence and Knowledge Sharing?* Master's thesis.

Chabrol, J.B.T., & von Bertalanffy, L. (1973). *General Theory of Systems*. Paris: Dunod.

Chatzoglou, P., Fragidis, L., Chatzoudes, D., & Symeonidis, S. (2016, September). Critical success factors for ERP implementation in SMEs. In *2016 Federated Conference on Computer Science and Information Systems (FedCSIS)* (pp. 1243–1252). IEEE.

Chausi, B. A., Chausi, A., & Dika, Z. (2016). Critical success factors in ERP implementation. *Academic Journal of Business, Administration, Law and Social Sciences, 2*(3).

Chew, W. B., Leonard-Barton, D., & Bohn, R. E. (1991). Beating Murphy's law. *MIT Sloan Management Review, 32*(3), 5.

Chirico, F., & Salvato, C. (2008). Knowledge integration and dynamic organizational adaptation in family firms. *Family Business Review, 21*(2), 169–181.

Chrisman, J. J. (2019). Stewardship theory: Realism, relevance, and family firm governance. *Entrepreneurship Theory and Practice, 43*(6), 1051–1066.

Chrisman, J. J., Chua, J. H., & Litz, R. A. (2002, December). Do family firms have higher agency costs than nonfamily firms. In *Second Annual Theories of Family Enterprises Conference, University of Pennsylvania.*

Chrisman, J. J., Hofer, C. W., & Boulton, W. B. (1988). Toward a system for classifying business strategies. *Academy of Management Review, 13*(3), 413–428.

Chua, J. H., Chrisman, J. J., & Sharma, P. (1999). Defining the family business by behavior. *Entrepreneurship Theory and Practice, 23*(4), 19–39.

Chung, C., Bozkurt, O., & Sparrow, P. R. (2012). Managing the duality of IHRM: Unravelling the strategy and perceptions of key actors in South Korean MNCs. *International Journal of Human Resource Management, 23*(11), 2333–2353.

Cieśla, B., & Kolny, D. (2019). Visual process analysis in SMEs as a support for management models on example of TOC. *Journal of Systems Integration, 10*(2), 19–27.

Clemons, C. (1998). Successful implementation of an enterprise system: a case study. *AMCIS 1998 proceedings*, 39.

Colli, A. (2006). *The History of Family Business, 1850–2000.* Cambridge: Cambridge University Press.

Colli, A. (2012). Contextualizing performances of family firms: The perspective of business history. *Family Business Review, 25*(3), 243–257.

Colli, A., & Perez, P. F. (2014). Business history and family firms. Sage Handbook of Family Firms, Sage, Londres, 269–292.

Company History, NTPC Limited. (2019). Retrieved from http://economictimes.indiatimes.com/ntpc-ltd/infocompanyhistory/companyid-12316.cms on 07.05.2019.

Computer Maintenance Corporation (2020). Extracted from http://cmcltd.com/ on 20.04.2020

Conant, J.S., Mokwa, M.P., & Varadarajan, P.R. (1990). Strategic types, distinctive marketing competencies and organizational performance: A multiple-measures-based study. *Strategic Management Journal, 11*(5), 365–383.

Crouse, P., Doyle, W., & Young, J. D. (2011). Workplace learning strategies, barriers, facilitators and outcomes: A qualitative study among human resource management practitioners. *Human Resource Development International, 14*(1), 39–55.

Damanpour, F. (1991). Organizational innovation: A meta-analysis of effects of determinants and moderators. *The Academy of Management Journal, 34*(3), 555–590.

Daniel, D. R. (1961). Management information crisis. *Harvard Business Review*, *39*(5), 111–121.

Dankert, C. E. (1948). *Contemporary Unionism*. New York: Prentice Hall.

Daspit, J. J., Holt, D. T., Chrisman, J. J., & Long, R. G. (2016). Examining family firm succession from a social exchange perspective: A multiphase, multistakeholder review. *Family Business Review*, *29*(1), 44–64.

Davenport, T. H. (1998). Putting the enterprise into the enterprise system. *Harvard Business Review*, *76*(4).

Davis, B., & Wilder, C. (1998). False starts, strong finishes: Companies are saving troubled IT projects by admitting their mistakes, stepping back, scaling back, and moving on. *Information Week*, *7*(11), 41–43.

Day, G.S. (1990). *Market Driven Strategy: Processes for Creating Value*. New York: Free Press.

de Holan, P. M., & Sanz, L. (2006). Protected by the family? How closely held family firms protect minority shareholders. *Journal of Business Research*, *59*(3), 356–359.

Delfmann, W., Albers, S., & Gehring, M. (2002). The impact of electronic commerce on logistics service providers. *International Journal of Physical Distribution & Logistics Management*, *32*(3), 203–222.

Dhanpat, N., Buthelezi, Z. P., Joe, M. R., Maphela, T. V., & Shongwe, N. (2020). Industry 4.0: The role of human resource professionals. *SA Journal of Human Resource Management*, *18*(1), 1–11.

DHL, Great Place to Work. (2020). Retrieved from www.greatplacetowork.in/great/profile/india-best/DHL-Supply-Chain on 02.02.2021.

Dicken, P. (1994). Global-local tensions: Firms and states in the global space-economy. *Advances in Strategic Management*, *10*, 217–247.

Dickmann, M., & Muller-Camen, M. (2006). A typology of international human resource management strategies and processes. *International Journal of Human Resource Management*, *17*(4), 580–601.

DiFonzo, N., & Bordia, P. (1998). A tale of two corporations: Managing uncertainty during organisational change. *Human Resource Management*, *37*(3), 295–303.

DiMaggio, P., & Powell, W. (1983). The iron cage revisited: Institutional isomorphism and collective rationality in organizational fields. *American Sociological Review*, *48*(2), 147–160.

Ding, B. (2018). Pharma industry 4.0: Literature review and research opportunities in sustainable pharmaceutical supply chains. *Process Safety and Environmental Protection*, *119*, 115–130.

Doeringer, P. B., Lorenz, E., & Terkla, D. G. (2003). The adoption and diffusion of high-performance management: Lessons from Japanese multinationals in the West. *Cambridge Journal of Economics*, *27*(2), 265–286.

Dolmetsch, R., Huber, T., Fleisch, E., & Österle, H. (1998). *Accelerated SAP: 4 Case Studies*.

Dowling, P.J., & Welch, D.E. (2004). *International Human Resource Management: Managing People in a Multinational Context* (4th ed.). London: Thomson.

Dowling, P., Festing, M., & Engles, A. (2008). *International Human Resource Management*. London: Thomson.

Doz, Y.L., & Hamel, G. (1998). *Alliance Advantage*. Boston, MA: Harvard Business School Press.

Doz, Y. L., & Prahalad, C. K. (1984). Patterns of strategic control within multinational corporations. *Journal of International Business Studies, 15*(2), 55–72.

D'Souza, E. (1998). World employment: ILO perspective. *Economic and Political Weekly*, 2537–2545.

Dyer Jr, W. G., & Wilkins, A. L. (1991). Better stories, not better constructs, to generate better theory: A rejoinder to Eisenhardt. *Academy of Management Review, 16*(3), 613–619.

eBay Inc (2020). Extracted from https://www.ebayinc.com/ on 20.04.2020

Education is a philanthropic effort and not business for us. *Financial Express*, 17 June 2012.

Edwards, H. M., & Humphries, L. P. (2005). Change management of people and technology in an ERP implementation. *Journal of Cases on Information Technology, 7*(4), 144–161.

Edwards, T. (2004). 15 The transfer of employment practices across borders in multinational companies. *International Human Resource Management*, 389.

Egan, R. W., & Fjermestad, J. (2005, January). Change and resistance help for the practitioner of change. In *Proceedings of the 38th Annual Hawaii International Conference on System Sciences* (pp. 219c–219c). IEEE.

Eisenhardt, K. M., & Graebner, M. E. (2007). Theory building from cases: Opportunities and challenges. *Academy of Management Journal, 50*(1), 25–32.

Eisenhardt, K. M., Graebner, M. E., & Sonenshein, S. (2016). Grand challenges and inductive methods: Rigor without rigor mortis. *Academy of Management Journal, 59*(4), 1113–1123.

Ellguth, P., & Kohaut, S. (2019). A note on the decline of collective bargaining coverage: The role of structural change. *Jahrbücher für Nationalökonomie und Statistik, 239*(1), 39–66.

Ensley, M. D., & Pearson, A. W. (2005). An exploratory comparison of the behavioral dynamics of top management teams in family and nonfamily new ventures: Cohesion, conflict, potency, and consensus. *Entrepreneurship Theory and Practice, 29*(3), 267–284.

Entrepreneur (2021). Extracted from https://www.entrepreneur.com/encyclopedia/family-businesses on 04.04.2021

Ericsson, Great Place to Work. (2020). Retrieved from www.greatplacetowork.in/great/profile/india-best/Ericsson-India on 02.02.2021

Esteves, J., & Pastor-Collado, J. (2000, November). Towards the unification of critical success factors for ERP implementations. In *10th Annual BIT Conference, Manchester, UK* (p. 44).

Esteves, J., & Pastor-Collado, J. (2001). Analysis of critical success factors relevance along SAP implementation phases. In *AMCIS 2001 Proceedings*, 197.

Etihad Airways (2020). Extracted from https://www.etihad.com/en-in/ on 20.04.2020

EY, Great Place to Work. (2020). Extracted from https://www.greatplacetowork.in/great/profile/india-best/ernst-and-young on 02.02.2021

Family Business.(2018). Retrieved from https://en.wikipedia.org/wiki/Family_business on 20.07.2018.

Farley, J.U., Hoenig, S., & Yang, J.Z. (2004). Key factors influencing HRM practices of overseas subsidiaries in China's transition economy. *International Journal of Human Resource Management, 15*(4–5), 688–704.

Farndale, E., Paauwe, J., Morris, S. S., Stahl, G. K., Stiles, P., Trevor, J., & Wright, P. M. (2010). Context-bound configurations of corporate HR functions in multinational corporations. *Human Resource Management, 49*(1), 45–66.

Ferraro, F., Etzion, D., & Gehman, J. (2015). Tackling grand challenges pragmatically: Robust action revisited. *Organization Studies, 36*(3), 363–390.

Fiss, P.C. (2009). Case studies and the configurational analysis of organisational phenomena. In D. S. Byrne & C. C. Ragin (Eds.), *The SAGE Handbook of Case-Based Methods* (pp. 424–440). Thousand Oaks, CA: Sage.

Follmer, E. H., Talbot, D. L., Kristof-Brown, A. L., Astrove, S. L., & Billsberry, J. (2018). Resolution, relief, and resignation: A qualitative study of responses to misfit at work. *Academy of Management Journal, 61*(2), 440–465.

Fonseca, A. J. (1964).*Wage Determination and Organized Labour in India.* Bombay: Oxford University Press.

Frederico, G. F., Garza-Reyes, J. A., Anosike, A., & Kumar, V. (2019). Supply Chain 4.0: Concepts, maturity and research agenda. *Supply Chain Management: An International Journal*, 1–21.https://doi.org/10.1108/SCM-09-2018-0339

Freeman, R., & Medoff, J. (1984). *What Do Unions Do?* New York: Basic Books.

Gagné, M. (2018). From strategy to action: Transforming organizational goals into organizational behavior. *International Journal of Management Reviews, 20*, S83–S104.

Gallo, M. A., & Villaseca, A. (1996). Financing family firms. *Family Business Review, 9*(4), 387–401.

Gates, L. P. (2010). *Strategic Planning with Critical Success Factors and Future Scenarios: An Integrated Strategic Planning Framework* (No. CMU/SEI-2010-TR-037). Pittsburgh, PA: Carnegie-Mellon University, Software Engineering Institute.

GE (2020). Extracted from https://www.ge.com/ on 20.04.2020

GE, Great Place to Work. (2020). Retrieved from www.greatplacetowork.in/great/profile/india-best/GE-India-Industrial on 02.02.2021.

Gedajlovic, E., Lubatkin, M. H., & Schulze, W. S. (2004). Crossing the threshold from founder management to professional management: A governance perspective. *Journal of management Studies, 41*(5), 899–912.

Geißler, A., Häckel, B., Voit, C., & Übelhör, J. (2019). Structuring the anticipated benefits of the fourth industrial revolution.

Ghemawat, P., & Hout, T. (2008). The global giants: Not the usual suspects. *Harvard Business Review, 86*(11), 80–88.

Ghobakhloo, M. (2018). The future of manufacturing industry: A strategic roadmap toward Industry 4.0. *Journal of Manufacturing Technology Management, 29*(6), 910–936.

Ghosh, P., & Geetika, C. (2007). Unionisation: A feasibility study for the Indian software industry. *Russian Management Journal, 5*(2), 45–56.

Ghoshal, S. (2003). Miles and snow: Enduring insights for managers. *The Academy of Management Executive, 17*(4), 109–114.

Ghoshal, S., & Bartlett, C.A. (1988). Creation, adaptation and diffusion of innovations by subsidiaries or multinational corporations. *Journal of International Business Studies, 19*(3), 365–388.

Glaser, B.G., & Strauss, A. L. (1967). *The Discovery of Grounded Theory: Strategies for Qualitative Research.* Chicago: Aldine Publishing Company.

General Motors (2020). Extracted from https://www.gm.com/ on 20.04.2020

Govindan, K., Palaniappan, M., Zhu, Q., & Kannan, D. (2012). Analysis of third party reverse logistics provider using interpretive structural modeling. *International Journal of Production Economics, 140*(1), 204–211.

Griffin, A., & Hauser, J.R. (1996). Integrating R&D and marketing: A review and analysis of the literature. *Journal of Product Innovation Management, 13*(2), 191–215.

Grzelczak, A., Kosacka, M., & Werner-Lewandowska, K. (2017). Employees competences for Industry 4.0 in Poland – Preliminary research results. *DEStech Transactions on Engineering and Technology Research.* https://doi.org/10.12783/dtetr/icpr2017/17598

Gunjal, S. (2019). Enterprise Resource Planning (ERP) as a change management tool. *Journal of Management, 6*(2).

Gunnigle, P., Murphy, K., Cleveland, J., Heraty, N., & Morley, M. (2001). Human resource management practices of US-owned multinational corporations in Europe: Standardization versus localization? *Advances in International Management, 14*, 259–284.

Gupta, S., & Bhaskar, A. U. (2016). Doing business in India: Cross-cultural issues in managing human resources. *Cross Cultural & Strategic Management, 23*(1), 184–204.

Haddara, M., & Elragal, A. (2015). The readiness of ERP systems for the factory of the future. *Procedia Computer Science, 64*, 721–728.

Hambrick, D.C. (1983). Some tests of the effectiveness and functional attributes of Miles and Snow's strategic types. *Academy of Management Journal, 26*(1), 5–25.

Hannon, J., Huang, I.C., & Jaw, B.S. (1995). International human resource strategy and its determinants: The case of subsidiaries in Taiwan. *Journal of International Business Studies, 26*(3), 531–554.

Harzing, A.W., & Sorge, A. (2003). The relative impact of country of origin and universal contingencies on internationalization strategies and corporate control in multinational enterprises: Worldwide and European perspectives. *Organization Studies, 24*(2), 187–214.

HCL Technologies (2020). Extracted from https://www.hcltech.com/ on 20.04.2020

Hetrick, S. (2002). Transferring HR ideas and practices: Globalization and convergence in Poland. *Human Resource Development International, 5*(3), 333–351.

HIL, Great Place to Work. (2020). Retrieved from www.greatplacetowork.in/great/profile/india-best/HIL-Ltd on 02.02.2021.

Hoglund, L. (2015). *Strategic Entrepreneurship: Organizing Entrepreneurship in Established Organizations.* Studentlitteratur AB.

Holland, C. P., Light, B., & Gibson, N. (1999). A critical success factors model for enterprise resource planning implementation. In *ECIS 1999: 7th European Conference on Information Systems* (pp. 273–287).

Hosain, M. S., Arefin, A. H. M. M., & Hossin, M. A. (2020). The role of human resource information system on operational efficiency: Evidence from MNCs operating in Bangladesh. *Asian Journal of Economics, Business and Accounting*, 29–47.

Hoxie, R. F. (1921). *Trade Unionism in the United States*. New York: Russel & Russel.

Hutchins, H. A. (1998). 7 key elements of a successful implementation and 8 mistakes you will make anyway. In *International Conference Proceedings-American Production and Inventory Control Society* (pp. 356–358). American Production and Inventory Control Society.

Infosys (2020). Extracted from https://www.infosys.com/ on 20.04.2020

InMobi, Great Place to Work. (2020). Retrieved from www.greatplacetowork.in/great/profile/india-best/InMobi-Technology-Services on 26.02.2021

Jackson, D. (1972). Wage policy and industrial relations in India. *The Economic Journal*, *82*(325), 183–194.

Jaguar Land Rover (2020). Extracted from https://www.jaguarlandrover.com/ on 20.04.2020

James, H. (2006). *Family Capitalism: Wendels, Haniels, Falcks and the Continental European Model*. Cambridge, MA: Belknap Press.

Jarzabkowski, P., & Fenton, E. (2006). Strategizing and organizing in pluralistic contexts. *Long Range Planning*, *39*(6), 631–648.

Jarzabkowski, P., & Kaplan, S. (2015). Strategy tools-in-use: A framework for understanding "technologies of rationality" in practice. *Strategic Management Journal*, *36*(4), 537–558.

Jensen, M. C., & Meckling, W. H. (1976). Theory of firm: Managerial behaviour, agency costs and ownership structure. *Journal of Financial Economics*, *3*(4), 305–360.

Jindal Steel & Power. (2019). Retrieved from www.jindalsteelpower.com on 16.04.2020.

John, S., & Chattopadhyay, P. (2020). A study on various elements of human resource management practices in different contexts: Theoretical approach. *Editorial Board*,*9*(2), 218.

Jose, A. V. (1999). *The Future of the Labour Movement: Some Observations on Developing Countries*. International Institute for Labour Studies.

Joshi, M., Dixit, S., Sinha, A. K., & Shukla, B. (2016). Conflicts in a family business: A case of Durga and Company. *Vision: The Journal of Business Perspective*, *22*(1), 105–110.

Joyce, P. (2004). Public sector strategic management: The changes required. *Strategic Change*, *13*(3), 107.

JSPL MD Naveen Jindal: A value creator and man of many passions. *The Economic Times*, 24 August 2012.

JSW Energy terminates Rs 6.5K deal to buy JSPL's 1 GW plant in Raigarh. *The Economic Times*, 1July 2019. Retrieved from https://economictimes.indiatimes.com/industry/energy/power/jsw-energy-terminates-rs-6-5k-deal-to-buy-jspls-1-gw-plant-in-raigarh/articleshow/70029524.cms?from=mdr on 16.04.2020.

JSW Energy to acquire JSPL's 1,000MW plant for Rs 6,500 crore. *Times of India*, 4 May 2016. Retrieved from http://timesofindia.indiatimes.com/business/india-business/JSW-Energy-to-acquire-JSPLs-1000MW-plant-for-Rs-6500-crore/articleshow/52108879.cms on 07.05.2019.

Kale, V. (2000). *Implementing SAP R/3: The Guide for Business and Technology Managers* (pp. 108–111). Carmel, IN: SAMS Publishing.

Kaplan, A. (1964). *The Conduct of Inquiry; Methodology in Behavioral Science*. San Francisco: Chandler Publications.

Karodia, N. C. (2018).*Managing the Transition to a 'Digital Culture': The Experience of Financial Service Firms*. Doctoral dissertation, University of Pretoria.

Keating, N. C., & Little, H. M. (1997). Choosing the successor in New Zealand family farms. *Family Business Review*, *10*(2), 151–171.

Kergroach, S. (2017). Industry 4.0: New challenges and opportunities for the labour market. *Foresight and Governance*, *11*(4), 6–8.

Kim, H. W. (2017). *The New Order of Workplaces: How Human Resource Management Has Changed Labor Unions in South Korea, 2005–2015*.Dissertation, Pennsylvania State University.

Kim, W. C., & Mauborgne, R. A. (1993). Procedural justice, attitudes, and subsidiary top management compliance with multinationals' corporate strategic decisions. *Academy of Management Journal*, *36*(3), 502–526.

Kopp, D. (2020). *Opinion | Loneliness Is a Health Hazard, Too*. Retrieved from www.wsj.com/articles/loneliness-is-a-health-hazard-too-11584906625 on 02.02.2021

Kostova, T. (1999). Transnational transfer of strategic organizational practices: A contextual perspective. *Academy of Management Review*, *24*(2), 308–324.

Kostova, T., Roth, K., & Dacin, M. T. (2008). Institutional theory in the study of multinational corporations: A critique and new directions. *Academy of Management Review*, *33*(4), 994–1006.

Kotter, J.P. (2008). *Corporate Culture and Performance*. New York: Simon and Schuster.

Kovach, K.A. (1995). Employee motivation: Addressing a crucial factor in your organization's performance. *Employee Relations Today*, *22*(2), 93–105.

Kovach, R.C. (1994). Matching assumptions to environment in the transfer of management. *International Studies of Management and Organization*, *24*(4), 83–99.

Kraemmergaard, P., & Rose, J. (2002). Managerial competences for ERP journeys. *Information Systems Frontiers*, *4*(2), 199–211.

Krishnan, R. (2016). *L&T Electrical and Automation Eyes Local Market to Drive Strong Business Growth*. Retrieved from www.business-standard.com/article/companies/l-t-electrical-and-automation-eyes-local-market-to-drive-strong-business-growth-116022000425_1.html on 07.05.2019.

Kristof, A. L. (1996). Person-organization fit: An integrative review of its conceptualizations, measurement, and implications. *Personnel Psychology*, *49*(1), 1–49.

Kristof-Brown, A. L., & Guay, R. P. (2011). Person–environment fit. In *APA Handbook of Industrial and Organizational Psychology, Vol 3: Maintaining, Expanding, and Contracting the Organization* (pp. 3–50). Washington, DC: American Psychological Association.

Kristof-Brown, A. L., Zimmerman, R. D., & Johnson, E. C. (2005). Consequences of individuals' fit at work: A meta-analysis OF person – job, person – organization, person – group, and person – supervisor fit. *Personnel Psychology, 58*(2), 281–342.

Krupp, J. A. (1998). Transition to ERP implementation. *APICS The PerformanceAdvantage,8*, 36–39.

Kumar, P., & Singh, R. K. (2012). A fuzzy AHP and TOPSIS methodology to evaluate 3PL in a supply chain. *Journal of Modelling in Management, 7*(3), 287–303.

Lansberg, I. (1999). *Succeeding Generations: Realizing the Dream of Families in Business*. Boston, MA: Harvard Business School Press.

La Porta, R., Lopez-de-Silanes, F., & Shleifer, A. (1999). Corporate ownership around the world. *The Journal of Finance, 54*(2), 471–517.

Latamore, G. B. (1999). Flexibility fuels the ERP evolution. *APICS The Performance Advantage, 9*(10), 44–51.

L&T(E&A). (2019). Extracted from http://www.larsentoubro.com/electrical-automation/ on 20.04.2020

L&T Sells its Electrical and Automation Business. (2020). Retrieved from https://mercomindia.com/lt-sells-electrical-automation-business/ on 17.04.2021.

Laughlin, S. (1999). An ERP game plan. *Journal of Business Strategy, 20*(1), 32–37.

Lawrie, G., Abdullah, N. A., Bragg, C., & Varlet, G. (2016). Multi-level strategic alignment within a complex organisation. *Journal of Modelling in Management, 11*(4), 889–910.

Lee, S., & Ahn, H. (2008). Assessment of process improvement from organizational change. *Information & Management, 45*(5), 270–280.

Lester, R. A., & Cannella, A. A. (2006). Inter-organisational families: How family firms use interlocking directorate to build community-level social capital. *Entrepreneurship: Theory and Practice, 30*(6),755–775.

Levitt, B., & March, J.G. (1988). Organizational learning. *Annual Review of Sociology, 14*(1), 319–338.

Lewis, L. K., & Seibold, D. R. (1998). Reconceptualizing organizational change implementation as a communication problem: A review of literature and research agenda. *Annals of the International Communication Association, 21*(1), 93–152.

Lezzi, M., Lazoi, M., & Corallo, A. (2018). Cybersecurity for Industry 4.0 in the current literature: A reference framework. *Computers in Industry, 103*, 97–110.

Lieb, R.C. (1992). The use of third-party logistics services by large American manufacturers. *Journal of Business Logistics, 13*(2), 29–42.

Löhde, A. S. K., Calabrò, A., & Torchia, M. (2020). Understanding the main drivers of family firm longevity: The role of business family learning. *International Studies of Management & Organization*, 1–23.

Lorange, P., & Johan, R. (1993). *Strategic Alliances: Formation, Implementation, and Evolution*. Cambridge, MA: Blackwell Business.

Losey, M.R. (1997). The future of HR professional: Competency buttressed by advocacy. *Human Resources Management, 36*(1), 147–150.

Lu, Y. (2017). Industry 4.0: A survey on technologies, applications and open research issues. *Journal of Industrial Information Integration, 6*, 1–10.

Lynch, C. F. (2002). 3PLs: The state of outsourcing. *Logistics Management, 41*(6), 47–47.

Lynham, S.A. (2000). Theory building in the human resource development profession. *Human Resource Development Quarterly, 11*(2), 159–178.

Madheswaran, S., & Shanmugam, K. R. (2003, July). Wage differentials between union and non-union workers: An econometric analysis. In *Presentation in the Far Eastern Meeting of the Econometric Society at Yonsei University* (pp. 4–6).

Magretta, J. (2011). *Understanding Michael Porter: The Essential Guide to Competition and Strategy*. Boston, MA: Harvard Business Press.

Mahadevan, H. (2000). Economic reforms and labour. In C.S. Venkataratnam & P. Sinha (Eds.), *Trade Union Challenges at the Beginning of 21st Century*. New Delhi: Indian Industrial Relations Association in association with Excel Books.

Mahindra & Mahindra (2020). Extracted from http://www.mahindra.com/ on 20.04.2020

Marasco, A. (2008). Third-party logistics: A literature review. *International Journal of Production Economics, 113*(1), 127–147.

Maxwell, K. (1999). Executive study assesses current state of ERP in paper industry. *Pulp and Paper, 73*(10), 39–43.

McCaskey, D., & Okrent, M. (1999). Catching the ERP second wave. *APICS: The Performance Advantage*, 34–38.

McDaniel, S.W., & Kolari, J.W. (1987). Marketing strategy implications of the Miles and Snow strategic typology. *Journal of Marketing, 51*(4), 19–30.

Melin, L., Johnson, G., & Whittington, R. (2003). Guest editors' introduction. Micro strategy and strategizing: Towards an activity-based view. *Journal of Management Studies, 40*(1), 3–22.

Meyer, B., & Biegert, T. (2019). The conditional effect of technological change on collective bargaining coverage. *Research & Politics, 6*(1).https://doi.org/10.1177/2053168018823957.

Miles, R. E., & Snow, C. C. (1978). *Organizational Strategy, Structure, and Process*. New York: McGraw-Hill.

Minahan, T. (1998). Enterprise resource planning. *Purchasing, 16*, 112–117.

Mishra, P., Shukla, B., & Sujatha, R. (2017). Changing contours of performance management paradigm. *International Journal of Applied Business and Economic Research, 15*(17), 353–371.

Mishra, P., Shukla, B., & Sujatha, R. (2018). Blue Dart and its HR: Global integration or local differentiation? *Journal of Management Research and Analysis, 5*(01), 292–304.

Mishra, P., Shukla, B., & Sujatha, R. (2019a). Vision actualisation and spirituality: A theoretical model. *Purushartha, 11*(02), 14–24.

Mishra, P., Shukla, B., & Sujatha, R. (2019b). Relevance of critical success factors in ERP-SAP implementation. Case of Odisha Power Generation Corporation, India. *Revista ESPACIOS, 40*(16).

Mitchell, R. K., Agle, B. R., Chrisman, J. J., & Spence, L. J. (2011). Toward a theory of stakeholder salience in family firms. *Business Ethics Quarterly, 21*(2), 235–255.

Mitchell, T. R. (1973). Motivation and participation: An integration. *Academy of Management Journal*, *16*(4), 670–679.

Moenaert, R.K., & Souder, W. E. (1996). Context and antecedents of information utility at the R&D/marketing interface. *Management Science*, *42*(11), 1592–1610.

Mohamed, M. Z. (1995). Innovation implementations in Malaysian firms: Process, problems, critical success factors and working climate. *Technovation*, *15*(6), 375–385.

Montgomery, C. A. (2012). *The Strategist: Be the Leader Your Business Needs*. New York: Collins.

Morris, M. H., Williams, R. O., Allen, J. A., & Avila, R.A. (1997). Correlates of success in family business transitions. *Journal of Business Venturing*, *12*(5), 385–401.

Motorola (2020). Extracted from https://www.motorola.in/home on 20.04.2020

Mukherji, A., Wright, P., & Mukherji, J. (2007). Cohesiveness and goals in agency networks: Explaining conflict and cooperation. *The Journal of Socio-Economics*, *36*(6), 949–964.

Murray, B. (2003). The succession transition process: A longitudinal perspective. *Family Business Review*, *16*(1), 17–33.

Muson, H. (2002). The Houghtons of Corning. *Families in Business*, *1*(6), 71–75.

Mustakallio, M., Autio, E., & Zahra, S. A. (2002). Relational and contractual governance in family firms: Effects on strategic decision making. *Family Business Review*, *15*(3), 205–222.

Myers, C. A. (1958). *Labor Problems in the Industrialization of India*. Cambridge, MA: Harvard University Press.

Myloni, B., Harzing, A.W.K.,& Mirza, H. (2004). Host country specific factors and the transfer of human resource management practices in multinational companies. *International Journal of Manpower*, *25*(6), 518–534.

Naim, M., Aryee, G., & Potter, A. (2010). Determining a logistics provider's flexibility capability. *International Journal of Production Economics*, *127*(1), 39–45.

NALCO. (2020). Retrieved from www.nalcoindia.com/ on 16.04.2020.

Nicholas Piramal Group (2020). Extracted from http://piramal.com/ on 20.04.2020

Nicholas Piramal Group (2020). Extracted from https://group.bnpparibas/en/ on 20.04.2020

Nikookar, G., Safavi, S. Y., Hakim, A., & Homayoun, A. (2010). Competitive advantage of enterprise resource planning vendors in Iran. *Information Systems*, *35*(3), 271–277.

Nimbalkar, S. A. (2019). Industrial relations of employees and management in the context of India: A study. *Journal of the Gujarat Research Society*, *21*(2), 567–572.

Nordqvist, M., Sharma, P., & Chirico, F. (2014). Family firm heterogeneity and governance: A configuration approach. *Journal of Small Business Management*, *52*(2), 192–209.

NSPCL (2020). Extracted from http://www.nspcl.co.in/ on 20.04.2020

NTPC. (2021). Retrieved from https://ntpc.co.in/ on 22.04.2021.

Oden, H., Langenwalter, G., & Lucier, R. (1993). *Handbook of Material and Capacity Requirements Planning*. New York: McGraw-Hill.

Odisha nixes Adani Plan. (2020). Retrieved from www.business- standard.com/article/companies/odisha-nixes-adani-plan-invokes-rofr-to-buy-aes-stake-in-power-project-120090901348_1.html on 09.03.2021

Odor, H. O. (2018). Organisational change and development. *European Journal of Business Management, 10*(7), 58–66.

ONGC (2020). Extracted from https://www.ongcindia.com/wps/wcm/connect/en/home/ on 20.04.2020

OPGC (2020). Extracted from http://www.opgc.co.in/ on 20.04.2020

Paik, Y., & Sohn, J.H.D. (2004). Striking a balance between global integration and local responsiveness: The case of Toshiba corporation in redefining regional headquarters' role. *Organizational Analysis, 12*(4), 347–359.

Pajo, K., & Cleland, J. (1997). *Professionalism in Personnel. The 1997 Survey of the HR Profession*. Wellington, New Zealand: Massey University.

Pandemics. (2020). Retrieved from www.webmd.com/cold-and-flu/what-are-epidemics-pandemics-outbreaks#1 on 02.02.2021

Parr, A. N., Shanks, G., & Darke, P. (1999). Identification of necessary factors for successful implementation of ERP systems. In *New Information Technologies in Organizational Processes* (pp. 99–119). Boston, MA: Springer.

Pattnaik, A. (2020). *Changing Role of Trade Union in Employee Relations in India*. Retrieved from www.pragatipublication.com/assets/uploads/doc/ca714-1138-1148.13679.pdf on 17.12.2020.

Perlman, S. (1928). *A Theory of Labour Movement*. New York: Macmillan.

Perlmutter, H. V. (1969). The tortuous evolution of the multinational corporation. *Columbia Journal of World Business,4*(1), 9–18.

Peterson, W. J., Gelman, L., & Cooke, D. P. (2001). ERP Trends. New York, NY: The Conference Board. Report 1292-01-RR.

Pfohl, H. C., Yahsi, B., & Kurnaz, T. (2015). The impact of Industry 4.0 on the supply chain. In *Innovations and Strategies for Logistics and Supply Chains: Technologies, Business Models and Risk Management. Proceedings of the Hamburg International Conference of Logistics (HICL)*(Vol. 20, pp. 31–58). Berlin: epubli GmbH.

Pinzone, M., Albe, F., Orlandelli, D., Barletta, I., Berlin, C., Johansson, B., & Taisch, M. (2020). A framework for operative and social sustainability functionalities in Human-Centric Cyber-Physical Production Systems. *Computers & Industrial Engineering, 139*, 105132.

Poister, T. H. (2010). The future of strategic planning in the public sector: Linking strategic management and performance. *Public Administration Review, 70*, s246–s254.

Porter, M. (1996). What is strategy. *Harvard Business Review*, November–December.

Porter, M.E. (1985). *The Competitive Advantage: Creating and Sustaining Superior Performance*. New York: Harvard Business Press.

Poza, E. J., & Messer, T. (2001). Spousal leadership and continuity in the family firm. *Family Business Review, 14*(1), 25–36.

PPL (2020). Extracted from http://www.paradeepphosphates.com/ on 20.04.2020

Prahalad, C.K., & Doz, Y. L. (1987). *The Multinational Mission: Balancing Global Demands and Global Vision*. New York: Free Press.

Pucik, V. (1992). Globalization and human resource management. In V. Pucik, N.M. Tichy, &C.K. Barnett (Eds), *Globalizing Management: Creating and Leading the Competitive Organization*. New York: John Wiley and Sons.

Quote Investigator. (2021). Retrieved from https://quoteinvestigator.com/2010/05/26/everything-counts-einstein/ on 15.02.2021

Rajan, R. G., & Zingales, L. (2001). The firm as a dedicated hierarchy: A theory of the origins and growth of firms. *The Quarterly Journal of Economics, 116*(3), 805–851.

Rajput, S., & Singh, S. P. (2018). Current trends in Industry 4.0 and implications in container supply chain management: A key toward make in India. In *Digital India* (pp. 209–224). Cham: Springer.

Rani, U., & Sen, R. (2018). Labour relations and inclusive growth in India: New forms of voice. In *Industrial Relations in Emerging Economies*. Edward Elgar Publishing.

Ratnam, C. S. V. (1999). India: Collective bargaining – workers are less committed to any solidarity based on ideology and will readily shift their allegiance if unions do not deliver results. *Labour Education*, 1–2.

Ratnam, C. S. V. (2006). *Industrial Relations*. New Delhi: Oxford University Press.

Ratnam, C. S. V. (2007). Trade unions and wider society. *Indian Journal of Industrial Relations*, 620–651.

Ready, D. A., Hill, L. A., & Conger, J. A. (2008). Winning the race for talent in emerging markets. *Harvard Business Review, 86*(11), 62–70.

Reksoatmodjo, W., Hartono, J., Djunaedi, A., & Utomo, H. (2012). Exploratory study on alignment between IT and business strategies. *International Journal of Business, 14*(2), 139–162.

Remesh, B. P. (2017). Informal work in the formal sector: Conceptualizing the changing role of the state in India. In *Critical Perspectives on Work and Employment in Globalizing India* (pp. 83–94). Singapore: Springer.

Richert, A., Shehadeh, M., Plumanns, L., Groß, K., Schuster, K., & Jeschke, S. (2016, April). Educating engineers for industry 4.0: Virtual worlds and human-robot-teams. Empirical studies towards a new educational age. In *2016 IEEE Global Engineering Education Conference (EDUCON)* (pp. 142–149). IEEE.

Rigby, D., & Bilodea, B. (2015). Management tools & trends. *Bain Brief*, June. Retrieved from www.bain.com/publications/articles/management-tools-and-trends-2015.aspx on 02.03.2021

RITES (2020). Extracted from https://www.rites.com/ on 20.04.2020

Robinson, B. (2020). *What Studies Reveal about Social Distancing and Remote Working During Coronavirus*. Retrieved from www.forbes.com/sites/bryanrobinson/2020/04/04/what-7-studies-show-about-social-distancing-and-remote-working-during-covid-19/?sh=4293036757e2 on 02.02.2021

Robinson, W. T., Fornell, C., & Sullivan, M. (1992). Are market pioneers intrinsically stronger than later entrants? *Strategic Management Journal, 13*(8), 609–624.

Roblek, V., Meško, M., & Krapež, A. (2016). A complex view of industry 4.0. *Sage Open, 6*(2), https://doi.org/10.1177/2158244016653987.

Rockart, J. F. (1979). Chief executives define their own data needs. *Harvard Business Review, 57*(2), 81–93.

Rosenzweig, P. M., & Nohria, N. (1994). Influences on human resource management practices in multinational corporations. *Journal of International Business Studies, 25*(2), 229–251.

Rothenberger, M. A., & Srite, M. (2009). An investigation of customization in ERP system implementations. *IEEE Transactions on Engineering Management, 56*(4), 663–676.

Ryan, J., & Gibbons, P. (2011). Reconciling pressures for integration and autonomy within multinational corporations: An examination of personnel policies and practices. *European Journal of International Management, 5*(6), 559–573.

Saam, N. J. (2007). Asymmetry in information versus asymmetry in power: Implicit assumptions of agency theory? *The Journal of Socio-Economics, 36*(6), 825–840.

Sahay, B. S., & Mohan, R. (2006). 3PL practices: An Indian perspective. *International Journal of Physical Distribution & Logistics Management, 36*(9), 666–689.

Salesforce, Great Place to Work. (2020). Retrieved from www.greatplacetowork.in/great/profile/india-best/Salesforce.com on 02.02.2021.

Sankaran, K. (2007). *Labour Laws in South Asia: The Need for an Inclusive Approach.* Geneva: ILO.

Santos, S. C., Santana, C., & Elhimas, J. M. C. (2018). Critical success factors for ERP implementation in sector public: An analysis based on literature and a real case. *ECIS Research Papers,* 180.

Sayeed, O. B., & Sinha, P. (1981). Quality of Working Life (QWL) in relation to job satisfaction and performance in two organizations. *Managerial Psychology, 2*(1), 15–30.

Schensul, S.L., Schensul, J.J., & LeCompte, M.D. (1999). *Essential Ethnographic Methods: Ethnographer's Toolkit.* Walnut Creek, CA: Altamira Press, Sage Publications.

Schragenheim, E. (2000). When ERP and TOC worlds collide. *APICS: The Performance Advantage, 10*(2), 54–57.

Schuler, R. S., Sparrow, P., & Budhwar, P. (2009). Major works in international human resource management. In P. Budhwar, R. Schuler, & P. Sparrow (Eds.), *Major Works in International Human Resource Management* (Vol. 1, pp. xxiii–xxviii). London, UK: Sage.

Schulze, W. S., Lubatkin, M. H., & Dino, R. N. (2003). Toward a theory of agency and altruism in family firms. *Journal of Business Venturing, 18*(4), 473–490.

Schweiger, D. M., & Denisi, A. S. (1991). Communication with employees following a merger: A longitudinal field experiment. *Academy of Management Journal, 34*(1), 110–135.

Sethi, D. (2009). Are multinational enterprises from the emerging economies global or regional? *European Management Journal, 27*(5), 356–365.

Shalini, T. R. (2020). Impact of rewards and recognition on employee commitment: A perspective of the bank employees. *LBS Journal of Management & Research, 18*(1), 10–16.

Shamim, S., Cang, S., Yu, H., & Li, Y. (2016, July). Management approaches for Industry 4.0: A human resource management perspective. In *2016 IEEE Congress on Evolutionary Computation (CEC)* (pp. 5309–5316). IEEE.

Shenkar, O., & Zeira, Y. (1987). Human resources management in international joint ventures: Directions for research. *Academy of Management Review, 12*(3), 546–557.

Sherrard, R. (1998). Enterprise resource planning is not for the unprepared. In *ERP World Proceedings*, August.

Shortell, S.M., & Zajac, E.J. (1990). Perceptual and archival measures of Miles and Snow's strategic types: A comprehensive assessment of reliability and validity. *Academy of Management Journal, 33*(4), 817–832.

Shrivastava, S. (2012). Identifying the major components of business communication and their relevance: A conceptual framework. *IUP Journal of Soft Skills, 6*(4), 51.

Sinha, K.K. (2014). *My Experiments with Unleashing People Power.* New Delhi: Blomsbury.

Sirmans, G. S., Sirmans, C. F., & Turnbull, G. K. (1999). Prices, incentives and choice of management form. *Regional Science and Urban Economics, 29*(2), 173–195.

Sishi, M., & Telukdarie, A. (2020). Implementation of Industry 4.0 technologies in the mining industry – a case study. *International Journal of Mining and Mineral Engineering, 11*(1), 1–22.

Sivathanu, B., & Pillai, R. (2018). Smart HR 4.0: How industry 4.0 is disrupting HR. *Human Resource Management International Digest, 26*(4), 7–11.

Sodhi, J.S. (1994). Emerging trends in industrial relations and human resource management in India industry. *Indian Journal of Industrial Relations, 30*(1), 19–37.

Sodhi, J.S. (1999). *Industrial Relations and Human Resources in Transition.* New Delhi: Shri Ram Centre for Industrial Relations and Human Resources.

Sparrow, P. R., & Budhwar, P. S. (1997). Competition and change: Mapping the Indian HRM recipe against world-wide patterns. *Journal of World Business, 32*(3), 224–242.

Spears, L. C. (2010). Character and servant leadership: Ten characteristics of effective, caring leaders. *The Journal of Virtues & Leadership, 1*(1), 25–30.

Stacho, Z., Stachová, K., Papula, J., Papulová, Z., & Kohnová, L. (2019). Effective communication in organisations increases their competitiveness. *Polish Journal of Management Studies, 19.*

Stedman, C. (1998). ERP can magnify errors. *Computerworld, 32*(42), 1–2.

Stefanou, C. (1999). Supply chain management (SCM) and organizational key factors for successful implementation of enterprise resource planning (ERP) systems. *AMCIS 1999 proceedings*, 276.

Stein, T. (1999). Making ERP add up – Companies that implemented enterprise resource planning systems with little regard to the return on investment are starting to look for quantifiable results. *Information Week, 735*, 59–63.

Stojkić, Ž., Veža, I., & Bošnjak, I. (2016). A concept of information system implementation (CRM and ERP) within Industry 4.0. In *Proceedings of the 26th DAAAM International Symposium* (pp. 912–919).

Suddaby, R., & Jaskiewicz, P. (2020). Managing traditions: A critical capability for family business success. *Family Business Review, 33*(3), 234–243.

Sumner, M. (1999, April). Critical success factors in enterprise wide information management systems projects. In *Proceedings of the 1999 ACM SIGCPR conference on Computer personnel research* (pp. 297–303).

Swanson, E.B. (1994). Information systems innovations among organizations. *Management Science, 40*(9), 1069–1092.

Syed, R., Bandara, W., French, E., & Stewart, G. (2018). Getting it right! Critical success factors of BPM in the public sector: A systematic literature review. *Australasian Journal of Information Systems, 22*.

Syntheite (2020). Extracted from http://www.synthite.com/synthite.html on 20.04.2020

Szulanski, G. (1996). Exploring internal stickiness: Impediments to the transfer of best practice within the firm. *Strategic Management Journal, 17*(S2), 27–43.

TATA MOTORS (2020). Extracted from https://www.tatamotors.com/ on 20.04.2020

TCS (2020). Extracted from https://www.tcs.com/ on 20.04.2020

Tayeb, M. (1998). Transfer of HRM practices across cultures: An American company in Scotland. *International Journal of Human Resource Management, 9*(2), 332–358.

Taylor, S., Beechler, S., & Napier, N. (1996). Toward an integrative model of strategic international human resource management. *Academy of Management Review, 21*(4), 959–985.

The Raymond Group (2020). Extracted from https://www.raymondgroup.com/ on 20.04.2020

Thomas, T. (2020). Retrieved from www.livemint.com/companies/news/l-t-sells-its-electrical-and-automation-business-to-schneider-electric-for-rs-14-000-crore-11598877278444.html on 17.04.2021.

Travis, D. (1999). Selecting ERP. *APICS: The Performance Advantage*, 37–39.

Tregoe, B.B., & Zimmerman, J.W. (1982). *Top Management Strategy*. London: John Martin Publishing.

Tsiga, Z. D., Emes, M., & Smith, A. (2016). Critical success factors for the construction industry. *PM World Journal, 5*(8), 1–12.

Tung, R. L., & Lazarova, M. (2006). Brain drain versus brain gain: An exploratory study of ex-host country nationals in Central and East Europe. *The International Journal of Human Resource Management, 17*(11), 1853–1872.

Ulku, M. A., & Bookbinder, J. H. (2012). Optimal quoting of delivery time by a third party logistics provider: The impact of shipment consolidation and temporal pricing schemes. *European Journal of Operational Research, 221*(1), 110–117.

Ulrich, D., Younger, J., & Brockbank, W. (2008). The twenty-first-century HR organization. *Human Resource Management, 47*(4), 829–850.

Veliu, L., & Manxhari, M. (2017). The impact of managerial competencies on business performance: SME's in Kosovo. *Journal of Management, 30*(1), 59–65.

Verbeke, A., Yuan, W., & Kano, L. (2019). A values-based analysis of bifurcation bias and its impact on family firm internationalization. *Asia Pacific Journal of Management*, 1–29.

Vollmer, H. M., & Mills, D. L. (1965). Some comments on" The professionalization of everyone?". *American Journal of Sociology*, 480–481.

Volwer, J. (1999). Learning in the play pit. *Computer Weekly, 27*, 34.

Walker, J. W. (1988). How large should HR staff be? *Personnel, 65*(10), 36.

Walker, O.C. Jr, Boyd, H.W. Jr, Mullins, J., & Larreche, J.C. (2003). *Marketing Strategy: Planning and Implementation* (4th ed.). Homewood, IL: Irwin/McGraw-Hill.

Walmart, Great Place to Work. (2020). Retrieved from www.greatplacetowork.in/great/profile/india-best/Walmart-India on 02.02.2021

Wee Kwan Tan, A., Yifei, Z., Zhang, D., & Hilmola, O. P. (2014). State of third party logistics providers in China. *Industrial Management & Data Systems, 114*(9), 1322–1343.

Weick, K.E. (1993). Organizational redesign as improvisation. In G. P. Huber & W.H. Glick (Eds.), *Organizational Change and Redesign* (pp. 346–379). New York: Oxford University Press.

Welles, E. O. (1995). There are no simple businesses anymore.*Inc.,17*(7), 66–74.

Westney, D. E. (1993). Institutionalization theory and the multinational corporation. In S. Ghoshal &E. Westney (Eds.), *Organization Theory and the Multinational Corporation* (pp. 53–76). London: Palgrave Macmillan.

Whysall, Z., Owtram, M., & Brittain, S. (2019). The new talent management challenges of Industry 4.0. *Journal of Management Development, 38*(2), 118–129.

Wilder-Smith, A., & Freedman, D. O. (2020). Isolation, quarantine, social distancing and community containment: Pivotal role for old-style public health measures in the novel coronavirus (2019-nCoV) outbreak. *Journal of Travel Medicine, 27*(2), taaa020.

Wright, P. M., & McMahan, G. C. (1992). Theoretical perspectives for strategic human resource management. *Journal of Management, 18*(2), 295–320.

Yaprak, A., & Karademir, B. (2010). The internationalization of emerging market business groups: An integrated literature review. *International Marketing Review, 27*(2), 245–256.

Yuan, Y., Lu, L. Y., Tian, G., & Yu, Y. (2020). Business strategy and corporate social responsibility. *Journal of Business Ethics, 162*(2), 359–377.

Zafft, R. J. (n.d.). When corporate governance is a family affair. *OECD Observer.* Retrieved www.oecdobserver.org/news/archivestory.php/aid/819/When_corporate_governance_is_a_family_affair.html on 15.11.2016.

Zahra, S. A., & Sharma, P. (2004). Family business research: A strategic reflection. *Family Business Review, 17*(4), 331–346.

Zander, U., & Kogut, B. (1999). Knowledge and the speed of the transfer and imitation of organizational capabilities. *Organization Science, 6*(1), 76–92.

Zhu, J. S. (2019). Chinese multinationals' approach to international human resource management: A longitudinal study. *The International Journal of Human Resource Management, 30*(14), 2166–2185.

Index

Note: Page numbers in italics indicate a figure and page numbers in bold indicate a table on the corresponding page.

Printed in the United States
by Baker & Taylor Publisher Services